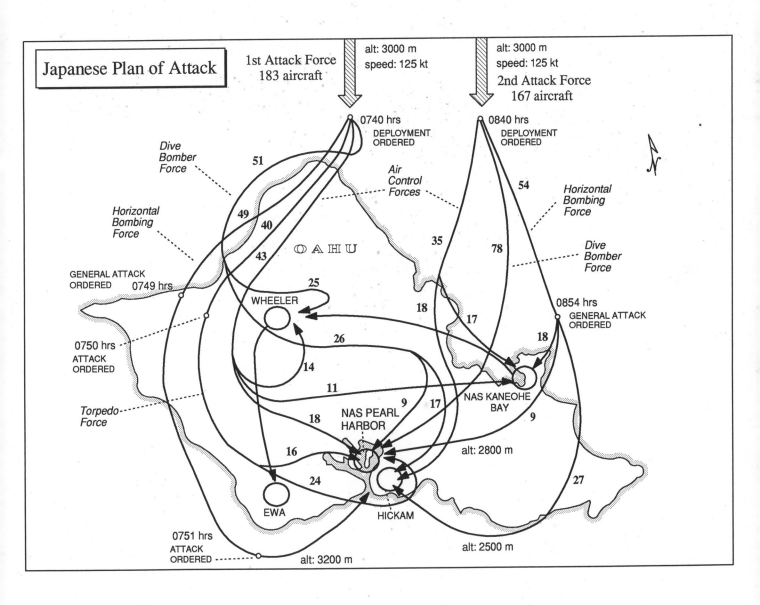

Japanese Plan of Attack

THE WAY IT WAS

PEARL HARBOR

Also by the Authors (with Gordon W. Prange)

At Dawn We Slept: The Untold Story of Pearl Harbor (1981)

Miracle at Midway (1982)

Target Tokyo: The Story of the Sorge Spy Ring (1984)

Pearl Harbor: The Verdict of History (1987)

December 7, 1941: The Day the Japanese Attacked Pearl Harbor (1988)

God's Samurai: Lead Pilot at Pearl Harbor (1990)

(with Masataka Chihaya)

Fading Victory: The Diary of Admiral Matome Ugaki (1991)

By J. Michael Wenger and Robert J. Cressman

Steady Nerves and Stout Hearts: The Enterprise (CV-6) Air Group at Pearl Harbor 7 December 1941 (1989)

THE WAY IT WAS
PEARL HARBOR
THE ORIGINAL PHOTOGRAPHS

DONALD M. GOLDSTEIN, KATHERINE V. DILLON
Coauthors of *At Dawn We Slept* and *Miracle at Midway*
and J. MICHAEL WENGER

BRASSEY'S (US), Inc.
A Macmillan Publishing Company

Washington • New York • London • Oxford
Beijing • Frankfurt • São Paulo • Sydney • Tokyo • Toronto

Book Design and Production by
Yaron Fidler

Brassey's (US), Inc.

Editorial Offices   *Order Department*
Brassey's (US), Inc.   Macmillan Publishing Co.
8000 Westpark Drive, 1st Floor   Front and Brown Streets
McLean, VA 22102   Riverside, NJ 08075

Maps by Albert D. McJoynt

Brassey's (US), Inc., books are available at special discounts for bulk
purchases for sales promotions, premiums, fund-raising, or educational
use through the Special Sales Director, Macmillan Publishing
Company, 866 Third Avenue, New York, New York 10022.

Library of Congress Cataloging-in-Publication Data
Goldstein, Donald M.
The way it was : Pearl Harbor—the original photographs / Donald
M. Goldstein, Katherine V. Dillon & J. Michael Wenger.
p.   cm.
ISBN 0-08-040573-8 (hardcover)
1. Pearl Harbor (Hawaii), Attack on, 1941—Pictorial works.
I. Dillon Katherine V. II. Wenger, J. Michael. III. Title.
D767.92.G65   1991   90-49572
940.54′26—dc20   CIP

British Library Cataloguing in Publication Data
The Way it was : Pearl Harbor : the original photographs.
1. Hawaii. Pearl Harbor. Air raids by Japan. Nihon Rikugun
K ok u-butaifa & Japan. Nihon Kaigun K ok u-bu, 1939-1945
I. Goldstein, Donald M. II. Dillon, Katherine V. III.
Wenger, J. Michael
940.5426

ISBN 0-08-040573-8

10   9   8   7   6   5   4   3

Published in the United States of America

Contents

Preface

J. Michael Wenger conceived *The Way It Was* more than ten years ago. A free-lance historian with an M.A. from Duke University, Wenger had become interested in Pearl Harbor and found many compelling pictures of that Day of Infamy. Encouraged by his wife and his good friend Robert J. Cressman, he continued collecting pictures for a possible book.

Two years later, at a convention in Pittsburgh, Wenger met Donald M. Goldstein, and they, along with the latter's collaborator, Katherine V. Dillon, agreed to cooperate in developing such a book. The result is a story told in photographs of what happened on Oahu on 7 December 1941.

Few military engagements have been so thoroughly captured on film. Indeed, everyone present with access to a camera seems to have been busily snapping away. With thousands of prints available, our problem was not finding significant prints but eliminating enough to keep the book to a reasonable size. The volume is organized into eight chapters and an epilogue. Chapter 1, "The Antagonists," introduces the key personnel; Chapter 2, "The Tools of War," describes the ships, aircraft, and weapons used; and Chapter 3, "The Setting," speaks briefly of the physical layout of Pearl Harbor and other military installations on Oahu. Chapter 4, "The Voyage to Hawaii," follows the Japanese task force as it moves toward Oahu; Chapter 5, "The Flight to Oahu," covers the flight of the attacking aircraft from their mother ships to their targets; Chapter 6, "The First Wave," briefly summarizes the stirring actions of the initial attack; and Chapter 7, "The Second Wave," does the same for the second and final assault. Chapter 8, "Panorama of Destruction," shows the desolation the Japanese left behind.

In this book the twenty-four-hour clock is used, in accordance with military custom; and abbreviations used are per Navy usage in 1941. Credits for individual photographs are noted very briefly, and a complete listing is given in the back of the book. The sharp-eyed reader will notice that in some cases an officer's rank as given in the text does not agree with the insignia on his uniform. The rank in the narrative is that held on 7 December, but in some cases contemporary photographs were not available, and those used may reflect subsequent promotions.

There is no bibliography. The text stems from the long experience of Goldstein and Dillon in working with the late Gordon W. Prange on his books about Pearl Harbor, which in turn were based upon a multiplicity of primary and secondary sources, as well as ships' logs, other material, and Japanese sources researched by Wenger. The reader interested in pursuing the subject is referred to the list of Prange's books at the front of this book.

We hope that this work will give the present-day reader some idea of *The Way It Was* on 7 December 1941.

We would like to dedicate this volume to the memory of Gordon W. Prange—historian, teacher, friend.

Acknowledgments

This book would have been impossible to put together without the cooperation of many people, both private citizens and those in official capacities. First, we wish to express deepest appreciation to Wenger's wife, Mary Ann, and his family, who stayed by him for all these years to the book's fruition. Special thanks are also due to Wenger's good friend Bob Cressman, who with him sought pictures for use in this book, and to Masataka Chihaya, formerly an officer in the Imperial Japanese Navy, for his advice and efforts on the Japanese part of the story. The collection of the late Gordon W. Prange yielded valuable pictures, thanks to his widow, Anne R. Prange.

Others who merit our sincere thanks are Al Makiel, a long-time collector of Japanese combat photography, who lent original pictures to be copied, and David Aiken, specialist in Japanese naval aviation and tactics. The following people also provided photographs and papers: M. Sgt. William M. Cleveland, USAF (Ret.); Kiyoko Egusa; M. Sgt. William E. Gemeinhardt, USMC (Ret.); Walter Lord; Col. Philip M. Rasmussen, USAF (Ret.); Lillian Sanders; and Robert F. Sumrall.

The following agencies provided their usual helpful cooperation. We are grateful to them and especially to their representatives: National Personnel Records Center—Richard M. Schrader; National Archives—Charles Gellert and James Trimble; and the Navy Historical Center—Charles Haberlein, Agnes F. Hoover, Kathy Lloyd, and Michael Walker. Others who helped were Richard F. Barnes, Jr.; Lt. Paul B. Conway, USN (Ret.); Comdr. David R. Permar, USCG (Ret.); and Michael Back.

Goldstein wishes to extend his personal appreciation to his wife, Mariann; his research assistant, Tom Muth; and Don McKeon, Christine Englert, and Vicki Chamlee for their help in putting the book together. We offer a special round of applause to Frank Margiotta, who had the guts to publish *The Way It Was*.

DONALD M. GOLDSTEIN,
PH.D.
Associate Professor of Public and
International Affairs
University of Pittsburgh
Pittsburgh, Pennsylvania

KATHERINE V. DILLON
CWO, USAF (Ret.)
Arlington, Virginia

J. MICHAEL WENGER,
M.A.
Raleigh, North Carolina

Introduction

Perhaps once or twice in a century, a nation undergoes an experience so unexpected, so shocking, so traumatic, that it splits life in two. Such an experience came to the United States on 7 December 1941, and ever after Americans alive on that day dated events as happening "before Pearl Harbor" or "after Pearl Harbor."

Of course, any thinking American who read the newspapers and listened to the newscasts knew that relations between Washington and Tokyo were very strained indeed. Japan had made no secret of its hostility—the Tripartite Pact was obviously aimed at the United States, and the government-controlled press fulminated against the Americans in season and out. Nor had Japan tried to conceal its designs on Southeast Asia, designs that might well have brought about a confrontation over the Philippines, then under the American flag. So, people may have had some suspicions that at some vague future date Japan and the United States would clash—but not in 1941, when Tokyo's ambassador and special envoy were in Washington holding conversations with Secretary of State Cordell Hull, and not at Pearl Harbor, a base widely touted as impregnable.

For that matter, many believed war with Japan would not occur anywhere, anytime. These people firmly held that the initiative lay with the United States and that no matter how far the Japanese might try American patience, they would never dare attack a nation so evidently superior in natural resources, manpower, industrial might, and military potential. Japan was not then the superpower it is in the 1990s. To a large segment of public opinion, Japan was less a real menace than a highly vocal nuisance that could be disregarded or put on the back burner while the country's attention focused on Europe. There, proud and ancient nations, birthplace to the ancestors of millions of Americans, struggled for life, lay conquered under the swastika, or had tied themselves ignominiously to the tail of Hitler's kite. In particular, American eyes watched, half hopefully, half fearfully, the titanic struggle under way in the Soviet Union between Hitler's thus far frighteningly successful mechanized hordes and the desperate Russians. Prognosticators had anticipated a German victory in six weeks; incredibly, the Russians were still holding on after nearly six months. No wonder that Japan, with its interminable war with China and its threats to the rest of Asia, seemed remote and of no direct application to the fate of the United States.

In fact, the Japanese and the Americans entertained serious and potentially lethal misconceptions about one another. Fundamental to American psychology and life-style were the principles that government existed to serve the people, that the civil arm should dominate the military—which was tolerated rather than honored—and that peace was inherently good. So Americans had difficulty relating to a culture in which the people believed they existed to support the power structure, the civil government kowtowed to the military, and war was considered a prideful manifestation of national manhood. Many Japanese firmly believed that their nation was destined to rule all Asia and that their national spirit, Yamato Damashii, gave them an enormous advantage over less virile peoples. Add to these factors an outsized persecution complex stemming from such factors as the naval treaties of the 1920s, U.S. immigration policies, and the embargoes of the summer of 1941, and the sum total resembles a volcano waiting to erupt.

For their part, a dangerously large number of Japanese honestly believed that the United States was vulnerable to Japanese aggression and that decades of prosperity and soft living had so declawed the American eagle that Japan could strike and secure whatever it wanted while Congress was still arguing about how to respond. Such mutual misunderstandings always contain the seeds of tragedy.

Needless to say, not all Japanese in high places deceived themselves that the Americans would be pushovers. One who acutely hoped to avoid trouble with the United States was Adm. Isoroku Yamamoto, commander in chief of the Combined Fleet. He had traveled and studied in that country and entertained a lively respect for its industry, its resources, and its people. When Premier Prince Fumimaro Konoye asked for Yamamoto's assessment of the Combined Fleet's capability vis-à-vis the American fleet in the event of war, he replied with characteristic honesty: he could "run wild" for six months, maybe a year, but he had no confidence for the long run. Yet ironically Yamamoto was the officer who planned the Pearl Harbor operation and pushed it through the reluctant Naval General Staff. His reasoning was that if Tokyo decided upon war the Combined Fleet would be the chief weapon. As its leader, he had to devise a strategy that might give his fleet the initial advantage that could make all the difference. He would strike not Pearl Harbor as such but the ships of the U.S. Pacific Fleet and the aircraft of the Hawaiian Air Force.

As a military operation, the attack was a Japanese victory. Psychologically, however, it was a Japanese disaster. Even Yamamoto, who in some respects understood the Americans quite well, failed to anticipate the reaction of blazing fury and grim resolve with which the United States met this unprovoked attack on its territory under the cover of peace discussions. The divisions of American aims upon which many Japanese counted—and some had been very real—coalesced into a single mighty objective. "Remember Pearl Harbor!" became the battle cry of the Pacific war.

The Americans were prey to other emotions, including bewilderment and hurt pride. How had the Japanese been able to take the "Gibraltar of the Pacific" by surprise? Some American or Americans must have been at fault, for the Japanese just could not be that good! So a search began that continued for years for someone on whom to pin responsibility. But the problem was much too complex for a simplistic solution.

Pearl Harbor taught—or should have taught—the United States many valuable lessons, perhaps chief among them never to underestimate the skill and resolution of any prospective opponent. Also demonstrated was the folly of assuming that people of a totally different culture would act in accordance with an American mentality. Moreover, the attack cruelly showed that no military post, however well manned and well armed, is any stronger than its state of alertness. Then, too, an old military principle had been violated, namely, that actions should be based upon a potential enemy's capabilities, not on an estimate of its intentions. The other lessons well worth pondering are too numerous to consider here.

The ranks of those who "remember that famous day and year" are thinning. To those born since 1941, Pearl Harbor is as remote as Yorktown, Gettysburg, or the Marne. Yet Americans must "remember Pearl Harbor," not to keep alive old hatreds, but to keep from forgetting the appalling price paid on that day and what could be payable in the future for smugness and psychological unpreparedness.

Here, then, is the story of Pearl Harbor told in pictures. Through them you will meet key people involved in the attack and the defense, become acquainted with the ships and aircraft, and above all, see the action as it happened. What no picture can quite convey, however, are the emotions—the astonishment, the horror, the anguish, the grief, and the consuming fury. For those you must call upon your imagination.

The Antagonists

As if a cosmic casting director had taken a hand, the leading characters in the Pearl Harbor drama were worthy of its awesome scope. No one can truly understand what happened at Pearl Harbor without at least a nodding acquaintance with these men, for the plan's inception, preparation, execution, and stunning success were shaped by the personalities and experience of those involved.

Because photographs exist of these individuals, they appear before the reader much as they did to their contemporaries, real people whose mentalities, strengths, and weaknesses have left their imprint on their features.

Of no one is this more true than of Adm. Isoroku Yamamoto (1–1). Without him, the Pearl Harbor plan never would have been possible. Born Isoroku Takano, he graduated from Japan's naval academy at Eta Jima in 1904 and then followed the usual pattern of any promising young naval officer. By 1916 he had become a lieutenant commander and been adopted into the Yamamoto family.

Some three years later, newly married, Yamamoto was ordered to the United States to attend courses at Harvard. There he picked up a good command of English and an addiction to poker. In December 1924, as a captain, he was appointed executive officer of the Navy's flight school at Kasumigaura. Under his dynamic leadership, Kasumigaura flourished, although to his sorrow the casualties were many.

In 1925 the Navy whisked him back to the United States for a two-year tour as naval attaché in Washington, D.C. After a quick spell of home duty, once again he went abroad, this time as a delegate to the London Naval Conference. Upon returning to Japan, he became commander of the First Carrier Division, a mutually profitable assignment. Yamamoto gained direct experience with carriers, and the naval aviators received the benefit of his drive and his insistence on their best performance.

Then, as a rear admiral, he headed Japan's delegation to the second London Naval Conference. There he maintained Japan's demands, which scuttled the conference, yet earned the respect of many of his opponents.

His next two assignments were in Tokyo, first as director of the Navy Ministry's Aeronautical Department, then as Navy vice minister. In the latter capacity he was so outspoken in his opposition to Japan's becoming involved with the Axis that the Navy Ministry packed him off to sea as commander in chief of the Combined Fleet, out of reach of the right-wingers who had threatened his life.

Thus at the outset of World War II in Europe, the Combined Fleet received a chief who had had very little high-level command or strategy experience but was unusually qualified to understand and appreciate the potential of naval aviation. When the crisis came, inevitably he thought in terms of carrier warfare. By January 1941, convinced that war with the United States and Great Britain was unavoidable, he outlined his Pearl Harbor plan in writing to the Navy minister and, typically, asked to lead the carrier force himself.

CHAPTER 1

1–1. Adm. Isoroku Yamamoto, commander in chief, Combined Fleet, originator of the plan to attack Pearl Harbor.

Throughout 1941, Yamamoto defended his concept in the face of all adverse arguments, which were many and potent. He finally ensured acceptance by threatening to resign if the Naval General Staff did not accept it. By that time the idea of going to war without him at the helm was unthinkable.

Yamamoto's good friend Rear Adm. Takijiro Onishi (1–2) was that rara avis, a real air admiral. He had won his wings in 1916, served as a seaplane pilot in World War I, tested parachutes for the Navy, and studied aerial warfare in England and France. He had served on many air staffs and consistently advocated the expansion of Japan's naval air power. He was not a particularly brilliant or original thinker, but he was a hard worker with a drive similar to Yamamoto's.

1–2. Rear Adm. Takijiro Onishi, chief of staff, Eleventh Air Fleet.

In January 1941 he was chief of staff of the land-based Eleventh Air Fleet and known for his ability to hammer out the details of tactical plans. Naturally Yamamoto called on him to work out the technical aspects and feasibility of the Pearl Harbor scheme. Although his own air officer declared the concept impossible, Onishi was not the man to give up easily. Together with his friend and disciple Comdr. Minoru Genda (1–3), he worked out the first operational draft. Onishi did not remain long at the heart of the Pearl Harbor planning. In fact, by early autumn he had ranged himself among the opponents of the plan.

Genda was another matter. No single person, not even Yamamoto, is more central to the Japanese side of the Pearl Harbor story. The admiral had the clout to put over the idea, but Genda had the knowledge to make it feasible.

After graduation from Eta Jima in 1924 and the mandatory training cruise, Genda turned to aviation and graduated from Kasumigaura in November 1929 at the head of his class. For six years he moved up the ladder of assignments and soon became known as one of Japan's ace fighter pilots. In addition to skill and courage, he had a brilliant, original mind full of ideas for naval air strategy and tactics, some so far ahead of their time that a number of his colleagues called him crazy.

At Yokosuka Air Corps as an instructor in 1934, Genda met Onishi, then the base executive officer. Onishi persuaded Genda to attend the Naval Staff College to prepare himself to fight for naval aviation at the top level. There his ideas included total reorganization of the Imperial Navy, with all battleships either scrapped or converted to carriers.

His next important assignment was as assistant naval attaché in London, where he studied British and European air power. When he left in September 1940, he took with him a great respect for British courage and determination, as well as serious reservations about Hitler's strategy and tactics. Home once more, he became air officer of the carrier *Kaga*, his position when Onishi brought him into the Pearl Harbor picture.

When on 10 April 1941 Japan organized the First Air Fleet, Genda was the obvious choice as air staff officer. In that capacity he worked on the Pearl Harbor plan from its inception, revising, refining, and probing for weaknesses. By the time the First Air Fleet sortied for the mission, most of Onishi's ideas had been deleted, and the final product clearly bore the hallmark of Minoru Genda.

In command of the First Air Fleet was Vice Adm. Chuichi Nagumo (1–4). He had behind him a long and honorable career as a specialist in torpedo warfare. His experience included service with battleships, cruisers, destroyers, and convoys in the Pacific during World War I. By 1935, as a rear admiral he had commanded successively a destroyer squadron and a heavy cruiser squadron, had seen war service in China, and had been president of the torpedo school at Yokosuka. Then he went back to sea as commander, Third Battleship Division. One year later he was promoted to vice admiral, and in November 1940 he became president of the Naval Staff College. He was serving in that position when the seniority system decreed that he assume command of the First Air Fleet.

Nagumo walked with a confident swagger and was generous and outgoing. A kindly man, he took a genuine interest in his subordinates. Recognizing his lack of experience in naval aviation, he relied heavily upon Genda and upon

1–3. Comdr. Minoru Genda, air staff officer, First Air Fleet.

1–4. Vice Adm. Chuichi Nagumo, commander in chief, First Air Fleet.

1–5. Rear Adm. Ryunosuke Kusaka, chief of staff, First Air Fleet.

1–6. Rear Adm. Tamon Yamaguchi, commander, Second Carrier Division.

his chief of staff, Rear Adm. Ryunosuke Kusaka (**1–5**). Kusaka never won his wings, but he had had several assignments in the air arm, including command of the carrier *Akagi.* In addition, his nature was placid, secure, and realistically optimistic.

Nagumo needed Kusaka's calm strength. Despite Nagumo's personal courage, when he learned of the Pearl Harbor scheme, he was appalled. It was the stuff of which an admiral's nightmares were made. The logistical problems alone seemed insurmountable. To the last possible moment, he argued against the plan and finally sortied with the gloomy conviction that he would lose a goodly proportion of his ships and men.

Nagumo commanded the First Carrier Division (*Akagi* and *Kaga*) as well as the First Air Fleet. Command of the Second Carrier Division (*Soryu* and *Hiryu*) fell to Rear Adm. Tamon Yamaguchi (**1–6**). Although enthusiastic about naval air power, he had little more experience in the field than Nagumo. He had a solid background in submarines and torpedo warfare, as well as the usual assortment of command and staff positions afloat and ashore. His assignments had taken him to the United States three times, the last occasion as naval attaché from 1934 to 1936. Four years later, as a rear admiral, he had his first direct naval air experience in command of the First Combined Air Corps. That same year, he moved over to the Second Carrier Division. In these positions his leadership was such that his fliers forgot that he was not one of them and gave him their unstinting admiration. The Pearl Harbor scheme, with all its boldness, even its open flirtation with death, dovetailed perfectly with Yamaguchi's personality, and he became an ardent champion of the plan.

The Fifth Carrier Division (*Shokaku* and *Zuikaku*) was under the command of Rear Adm. Chuichi Hara (**1–7**). He was a latecomer to the Pearl Harbor picture because his division was not activated until completion of *Zuikaku* on 25 September. Very proud of his command, he rated his carriers as the best in the Imperial Navy. His air crews were inexperienced, however, compared to the veterans of the other divisions.

Like Nagumo, Hara was a torpedo expert. A heavy man, Hara's friends called him "King Kong." He had a clear, incisive mind. Although he seriously questioned the wisdom of fighting the United States, once Yamamoto decided on the Pearl Harbor operation, Hara believed that the First Air Fleet should do its best to carry it out.

Vice Adm. Gunichi Mikawa (**1–8**) commanded the Pearl Harbor Support Force, consisting of the Third Battleship Division (*Hiei* and *Kirishima*) and the Eighth Heavy Cruiser Division (*Tone* and *Chikuma*). He agreed with the Pearl Harbor plan to this extent: Japan could not match the United States in sea power, shipbuilding, or industrial might. Its only chance was to strike the U.S. Pacific Fleet at the outset and quickly occupy the resource-rich area of Southeast Asia. Then Japan would be able to wage a long war. However, he realized that carrying out the Pearl Harbor attack at the same time as the southern operations meant overextending the Japanese Navy's capabilities. He also worried because he did not have his full complement of battleships. *Haruna* and *Kongo* had been detached from his division to serve elsewhere. A solid battleship admiral, Mikawa considered two such vessels wholly inadequate, should the task force encounter the American surface fleet at sea.

Another support organization was the First Destroyer Squadron (light cruiser *Abukuma* and nine destroyers) un-

1–7. Rear Adm. Chuichi Hara, commander, Fifth Carrier Division.

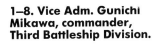

1–8. Vice Adm. Gunichi Mikawa, commander, Third Battleship Division.

der Rear Adm. Sentaro Omori (1–9). As with a number of the high-ranking participants in the Pearl Harbor venture, Omori was a torpedo expert. He and Mikawa did not learn of the Pearl Harbor project until the war games in September 1941.

When Omori assumed command of the squadron in November 1940, it was made up of old types of vessels, but the Pearl Harbor plan changed all that. By the time the task force was ready, Omori had the newest and best destroyers in the Imperial Navy. Nevertheless, destroyers were short-range ships, and Omori's greatest worry was getting them to Oahu and back. This problem necessitated unremitting training in refueling, not only from tankers but also from battleships and carriers if necessary. En route to Oahu, Omori also fretted over possible detection by the U.S. Navy. He believed that a combined U.S. air, surface, and submarine attack could have inflicted heavy damage on his task force.

Rear Adm. Shigeyoshi Miwa (1–10) commanded the Third Submarine Squadron of nine submarines. Because they would have to refuel in the Marshall Islands, Miwa's submarines left Japan on 11 November. Two of them, *I–72* and *I–73*, were scheduled to scout the Lahaina area. Another submarine, *I–74*, was to lie off Niihau and rescue any fliers in distress. Then, too, the Second Submarine Division (*I–19*, *I–21*, and *I–23*) accompanied the task force as a rear guard.

All this surface and undersea power was in support of the airmen, so the man who would lead them into battle was a key member of the Pearl Harbor team. Genda insisted that he wanted Comdr. Mitsuo Fuchida (1–11), his Eta Jima classmate, and no other to spearhead the attack. Their careers had run neck and neck, although Fuchida was a bomber pilot, not a fighter pilot. Genda knew him to be both an inspirational leader and a good staff officer.

Fuchida came to the First Air Fleet in late August and plunged into directing an intensive training program, but about a month passed before he was briefed on his mission. Thereafter, he participated in the planning as well as the preparations for the attack. On 7 December, he was overall air commander of the first wave and also headed the high-level bombing attack. Remaining throughout the second wave as an observer, he was the last flier to leave the area.

The American side of the story offered characters fully as

1–9. Top: Rear Adm. Sentaro Omori, commander, First Destroyer Squadron.

1–10. Top Right: Rear Adm. Shigeyoshi Miwa, commander, Third Submarine Squadron.

1–11. Right: Comdr. Mitsuo Fuchida, commander of aircraft, First Air Fleet and *Akagi*'s air group commander.

interesting, experienced, and capable as the Japanese. Adm. Husband E. Kimmel, commander in chief, U.S. Pacific Fleet (CinC PAC) (1–12), had many characteristics in common with Yamamoto, although he lacked Yamamoto's charisma and creative imagination. He graduated from Annapolis in 1904, the same year Yamamoto graduated from Eta Jima. Kimmel soon revealed a remarkable talent for gunnery, and many of his early assignments were connected with that field.

As he moved along his career channel—always intelligent, forthright, and awesomely diligent, demanding much of his subordinates and more of himself—his superiors realized that he was a man to watch. In May 1925 Kimmel was selected to attend the Naval Staff College. Soon after graduation, he was promoted to captain and sent to head-

1–12. Adm. Husband E. Kimmel, commander in chief, Pacific Fleet (center), flanked by his operations officer, Capt. Walter S. DeLany (left), and his chief of staff, Capt. William Ward ("Poco") Smith (right).

quarters in Washington in the Policy and Liaison Division. After three years there, he returned to sea in command of Destroyer Squadron Twelve and then for two years worked as director of ship movements in Washington, where he was tabbed "a humdinger." His next position, command of the battleship *New York,* was followed by assignment in the Navy Department as its budget officer. While there he became a rear admiral, and, some eight months later, in July 1938, he returned to sea in command of Cruiser Division Seven. Within a year he had stepped up to commander, Cruisers, Battle Force.

This stainless career involved no experience with naval aviation. Kimmel's natural habitat was the bridge of a battleship. Yet, when in February 1941 he assumed command of the U.S. Pacific Fleet with the rank of full admiral, he sensibly moved Fleet Headquarters from the flagship *Pennsylvania* to a shore location at Pearl Harbor. There he assembled an unusually able staff of officers who, like Yamamoto's official family, were almost fanatically loyal to their chief.

Kimmel was devoted to the offensive; he never visualized his fleet as taking a defensive posture. Throughout 1941 he worked himself and everyone else to the verge of exhaustion to prepare for the day when his ships would sail forth to engage the enemy. After the debacle, ironically enough, the U.S. Pacific Fleet's ships and men were generally conceded to have never been in better fighting trim than under Kimmel's leadership.

Events pushed Kimmel into command of the fleet unexpectedly. His predecessor, Adm. James O. Richardson (1–13), had incurred the wrath of President Roosevelt, and the Navy had to pick a successor a full year before a normal change. When in the early spring of 1940 the U.S. Pacific Fleet was stationed in Hawaiian waters, ostensibly as a deterrent to Japan, Richardson disapproved strongly and carried his opposition to the White House. He believed that the fleet was not ready for war, and he had a number of objections to Pearl Harbor, although danger to the fleet was not among them. He pushed Roosevelt too far and was relieved after only one year as CinC PAC, not, however, before he had established two dangerous precedents: he put the fleet on an operating schedule so fixed that its movements were readily predictable, and he considered torpedo nets around his ships an unnecessary precaution.

Richardson had established his fixed operating schedule at the request of Rear Adm. Claude C. Bloch (1–14). As commandant, Fourteenth Naval District, Bloch was in charge of operating the base at Pearl Harbor, as well as other U.S. Pacific bases. He wanted a predictable fleet movement in and out of the harbor so the ships would not interfere with dredging. Bloch had preceded Richardson as CinC US and was in Hawaii on his final tour of duty before retirement. In normal peacetime, the job could have been considered a pleasant, not too onerous post, but in 1941 Bloch had serious responsibilities. Although the Hawaiian Department of the U.S. Army was charged with protecting the bases and the ships in the harbor, Bloch was responsible for the Navy's share of these measures, including long-range aerial reconnaissance.

Second in seniority to Kimmel at Pearl Harbor was Vice Adm. William S. Pye (1–15), commander, Battle Force. Pye was considered a brilliant strategist and would function as CinC PAC if for any reason Kimmel could not. Because his battleships suffered most heavily from the attack, 7 December 1941 would be a particularly tragic day for Pye.

Whenever Kimmel's duties touched upon naval aviation, he usually consulted with his good friend and academy class-

1–14. Rear Adm. Claude C. Bloch, commandant of the Fourteenth Naval District.

1–13. Adm. James O. Richardson, Kimmel's predecessor.

1–15. Vice Adm. William S. Pye, commander, Battle Force.

mate, Vice Adm. William F. Halsey (**1–16**). Like Yama-guchi, Halsey had an aggressive, swashbuckling personality and a knack for winning the hearts of his officers and men. Unlike Yamaguchi, however, he was the real thing in air admirals who had learned to fly at Pensacola at the age of fifty-one. He was later one of the great heroes of the Pacific war, but his part in Pearl Harbor was tangential.

When Halsey took his first flight, back in 1913, the pilot was Patrick N. L. Bellinger (**1–17**). Now a rear admiral, Bellinger was in Hawaii with primary duty as commander, Patrol Wing Two. In that capacity he had charge of the PBY patrol aircraft based in Hawaii. Like Onishi, Bellinger had been an airman from the beginning, and his record bulged with Navy firsts in the field. He had a pleasant disposition that won him many friends.

Lt. Gen. Walter C. Short (**1–18**, shown with Kimmel, Capt. Lord Louis Mountbatten, Bellinger, and Maj. Gen. Frederick L. Martin), commanding general, Hawaiian De-partment, technically was Bloch's opposite, but, as the top Army officer present, most of his direct contacts were with Kimmel. Short was atypical for a general officer in not being a West Pointer. Since receiving a direct commission in 1902, he had served with infantry regiments at various stateside posts, in the Philippines and Alaska, and with the Pershing expedition to Mexico. World War I took him to France as a captain in various training capacities, and he participated in several battles.

Back in the peacetime Army, he served several tours of duty in Washington, graduated from the Army War Col-lege, and went to Puerto Rico for three years. By 1937 he had won his first star and served well in command assign-ments. Chief of Staff George C. Marshall was confident that Short was the logical man to assume command in

1–16. Vice Adm. William F. Halsey, commander, Aircraft, Battle Force.

1–17. Rear Adm. Patrick N. L. Bellinger, commander, Patrol Wing Two.

Hawaii. Indeed, he was competent and conscientious and worked hard to improve his organization. He established cordial relations with Kimmel. Oddly enough, however, although Marshall had spelled out to Short in unmistakable terms that the Hawaiian Department's primary duty was to protect the fleet in Hawaii, Short looked upon the fleet as protection for the islands and believed that the Japanese would attack, if at all, only were the fleet at sea well away from Hawaii.

Under Short's overall air command was the Hawaiian Air Force, led by Maj. Gen. Frederick L. Martin (**1–19**). In 1941 he was fifty-eight years old and had been a flier for nineteen years. The Army Air Corps's senior pilot and

1–18. Lt. Gen. Walter C. Short, commanding general, Hawaiian Department (left), with Kimmel (right), Capt. Lord Louis Mountbatten (center), Maj. Gen. Frederick L. Martin, and Bellinger in September 1941.

1–19. Maj. Gen. Frederick L. Martin, commanding general, Hawaiian Air Force.

1–20. Brig. Gen. Jacob H. Rudolph, commanding general, Eighteenth Bombardment Wing, as a major.

1–21. Brig. Gen. Howard C. Davidson, commanding general, Fourteenth Pursuit Wing, in 1945.

technical observer, he had two thousand hours of flight time to his credit. He came to Hawaii under orders to smooth interservice relations and worked hard to that end. With Bellinger he issued the famous Martin-Bellinger Report, which scarcely could have estimated Japan's intentions better had they read Yamamoto's mind. Yet personally Martin doubted that the Japanese would try to attack Oahu.

Martin's two major subordinate commanders were Brig. Gen. Jacob H. Rudolph, commanding general, Eighteenth Bombardment Wing (1–20), and Brig. Gen. Howard C. Davidson, commanding general, Fourteenth Pursuit Wing (1–21). Both Rudolph's bombers and Davidson's fighters were engaged primarily in training during 1941.

All these men, Americans and Japanese, of such varied experiences and personalities, had certain things in common. None was actuated by greed for either wealth or personal power. All were sincere patriots and dedicated officers who were striving to do their respective duties to the best of their abilities. The mistakes they made were made in good faith. Stars or supporting players, they made a good cast.

The Tools of War

Just as a photograph transforms an individual from a name to a person, so pictures of major military hardware enable the reader to visualize the action as it unfolds.

Commodore Matthew Perry was the unwitting father of the modern Imperial Japanese Navy. When he opened Japan in 1853, an intelligent, energetic people emerged into a world dominated by sea power and into a political climate attuned to the concept of empire. The Japanese decided that if they must live in this world they would live in it well. That decision meant having a first-class navy.

The world learned how well they had succeeded in the Sino-Japanese and Russo-Japanese wars. Even before World War I, Japan considered the U.S. Navy its prime rival in the Pacific. Despite Japan's devotion to the offensive, however, its war plans did not include attacking the U.S. Navy in its own waters. Its strategy was the so-called Great All-Out Battle, by which the Japanese would lure the Americans near the home islands and then annihilate them. Because the Japanese did not visualize fighting at a distance from their home bases, until the start of the "Chinese Incident" they lacked the necessary fleet train to make such a venture practical. This mind-set helps to explain the level and intensity of the opposition to Operation Hawaii.

By 1941, however, Japan had ships of the caliber to make the project possible. Because Nagumo's flagship, *Akagi* (**2–1**), had been laid down as a battle cruiser, she bore the name of a mountain instead of a flying creature, as did most Japanese carriers. She carried eighteen fighters, eighteen dive-bombers, and twenty-seven high-level or torpedo bombers. She had the disadvantage of a relatively short radius of action. If refueling had proved impossible, *Akagi* would have had to return to Japan. *Akagi* and *Kaga* were roughly comparable to Kimmel's *Saratoga* and *Lexington* but slightly slower. The U.S. flattops could make thirty-four knots to *Akagi*'s thirty-one and *Kaga*'s twenty-eight; however, these Japanese carriers were superior to their American counterparts in armament and tonnage.

Kaga (**2–2**) boasted the most impressive combat record of all Japanese carriers. She made up for her slightly slower speed with an immense fuel capacity. Because she had been converted from a battleship, she was named for one of Japan's ancient provinces. She carried the same complement of aircraft as *Akagi*. *Kaga*'s crew considered her a happy ship with a lucky presence.

Soryu ("blue dragon"), flagship of the Second Carrier Division (**2–3**), was the first large carrier Japan constructed from the keel up. Completed in 1937, she became, with modifications, the pattern for a number of future carriers, including *Hiryu* ("flying dragon"), which was completed in 1939. *Hiryu* (**2–4**) was readily identifiable by the island superstructure located amidships on the port side. Both ships were combat veterans, *Soryu* having participated in the invasion of Hainan in 1939 and the two having teamed

2–1. The aircraft carrier *Akagi*, flagship of the Pearl Harbor Strike Force.

2–3. *Soryu*, lead ship in the Second Carrier Division.

2–2. *Kaga,* companion to *Akagi* in the First Carrier Division.

2–4. *Hiryu* of the Second Carrier Division.

up for the occupation of French Indochina in July 1941. Each could make a maximum speed of thirty-four knots; so could their nearest U.S. equivalent, *Enterprise.* However, *Enterprise* alone could loft some eighty-five aircraft; the combined air strength of *Soryu* and *Hiryu* was 108, the individual complement of fifty-four being divided equally between fighters, dive-bombers, and high-level or torpedo bombers. The Second Carrier Division's main handicap was small fuel capacity—only seven thousand tons combined—which made Yamaguchi's flattops totally dependent upon refueling. For this reason, the Second Carrier Division's participation in Operation Hawaii was by no means certain until quite late in the planning.

Shokaku ("flying crane"), flagship of the Fifth Carrier Division (2–5), and *Zuikaku* ("glorious crane," 2–6) were so new that the voyage to Hawaii was their shakedown cruise. Commissioned in August and September 1941, respectively, their action radius was such that they could reach Oahu and return to Japan without refueling. Each carried eighteen fighters, twenty-seven dive-bombers, and twenty-seven high-level bombers. These carriers' weakness was unseasoned flight crews, but war quickly cured that condition.

The flagship of the Pearl Harbor Support Force was *Hiei* (2–7). Her crew was especially proud because this ship was known to be Emperor Hirohito's favorite. She and the *Kirishima* (2–8) were able to make the voyage to Hawaii and back without refueling. Their keels had been laid before World War I as battle cruisers, so they were named after mountains; however, they were officially classed as battleships. Sleekly built, they could make almost thirty knots— some eight or nine faster than the U.S. battleships—but their belt armor was much thinner and they carried eight 14-inch guns, whereas battleships in the Maryland class carried an equal number of 16-inchers.

The heavy cruisers *Tone* (2–9) and *Chikuma* (2–10) could make a speed of almost thirty-six knots. They carried eight 8-inch guns—one fewer than Kimmel's heavy cruisers —but had six 24-inch, oxygen-fueled torpedo tubes, which the American heavy cruisers did not. The skipper of *Chikuma* considered his ship "a match for anything afloat in 1941."

Like all Japanese light cruisers, *Abukuma* (2–11), flagship of the destroyer screen, derived her name from a river. The nine destroyers she led were excellent, most of them larger and stronger than anything the United States had at

2–5. *Shokaku,* flagship of the Fifth Carrier Division.

2–6. *Zuikaku* of the Fifth Carrier Division.

2–8. *Kirishima* of the Pearl Harbor Support Force.

2–7. *Hiei,* flagship of the Pearl Harbor Support Force.

2–9. The heavy cruiser _Tone._

2–10. The heavy cruiser _Chikuma._

2–11. The light cruiser _Abukuma,_ flagship of the First Destroyer Squadron.

Pearl Harbor. Examples of these destroyers were *Isokaze* ("wind of the seashore," **2–12**) and *Shiranuhi* ("will-o'-the-wisp," **2–13**). They could not quite match the 36.5-knot speed of the lighter American destroyers.

The flattops that fought at Pearl Harbor carried three types of attack aircraft. The fighters (*kansen*) were the Mitsubishi A6M2 Type 00 Zero-Sen (**2–14**). The Americans code-named it "Zeke," but the name did not stick. This fighter was the fabulous Zero, and the name was all too appropriate; nothing could match it in the first year of the Pacific war. At its cruising speed of 240 miles per hour, its range, loaded, was 790 miles. It carried two 7.7-millimeter machine guns and two 20-millimeter wing cannons. The Zero sacrificed safety measures to secure speed and maneuverability, so the Zero was exceedingly vulnerable—if its opponent could catch up to it.

Nagumo's dive-bombers were the Aichi D3A1 Type 99 (*kanbaku*) (**2–15**), nicknamed "Val." It was Japan's workhorse dive-bomber. It carried a crew of two with a bomb load of more than five hundred pounds and three 7.7-millimeter machine guns. The heavy-looking "spats" over its main landing gear gave it an awkward appearance; however, it stood comparison with the U.S. Navy's Douglas SBD Dauntless.

Most of the Japanese aircraft that attacked Oahu were Nakajima B5N2 Type 97 bombers (*kanko*, **2–16**), aka "Kate." The Japanese used them as both high-level and torpedo bombers. These planes carried a crew of three and an 800-kilogram torpedo or the equivalent in bombs (**2–17** and **2–18**). Kate had a comparatively slow cruising speed of 160 miles per hour, with a cruising range at that speed, when loaded, of 1,060 miles. The torpedoes gave the Japanese the most trouble in preparing for Operation Hawaii. Special technical adjustments had to be invented and attached to the torpedoes, and the crews of the torpedo bombers had to train exhaustively before they could drop the torpedo into Pearl Harbor's shallow water with any certainty that it would run rather than plunge into the mud.

To those aboard the U.S. ships in Pearl Harbor, especially the regular Navy complement, their vessel was more than a floating conglomeration of engines, armament, and living quarters—it was home. Moreover, each ship had a distinctive personality. So the sinking or damaging of a ship meant more to her men than the loss of an instrument of war; it was a blow to the psyche.

2–12. *Isokaze,* **a destroyer.**

2–13. *Shiranuhi* **takes on fuel from a tanker.**

2–14. A "Zero" from *Akagi.*

2–15. A "Val" from *Akagi.*

2–16. A "Kate" from *Akagi.*

2–17. Type 91 Kai Model 2 torpedoes rest on board *Akagi*'s flight deck. Note *Hiryu* in the background.

2–18. Type 99 Number 80 Mark III bomb.

The battleships at their moorings that morning of 7 December 1941 as they appeared in their pre-attack pride were of fairly antique vintage. However, they were well kept and most impressive, especially because in the latter months of 1941 they had received new paint jobs in camouflage styles called "measures." *California* (2–19), completed in 1921, was the flagship of Pye's battle force. She had the color scheme Measure 1, the usual camouflage—that is, dark gray to the funnel tops and light gray above.

Oklahoma (2–20), completed in 1916, was the last U.S. battleship built with reciprocating engines rather than turbines; she was the least modern of the battleships in Pearl Harbor on 7 December 1941. Although mandatory splinter shielding protected her antiaircraft battery, she had rather less than her comrades. The men who enlisted in her tended to stay rather than transfer. As one remarked, *Oklahoma* was "a clean, happy ship with a lot of spirit."

One of the oldest vessels in Pearl Harbor on that day was the ex-battleship *Utah* (2–21), completed in 1909 and long since downgraded to a target ship. However, she was not a mere empty shell; she was also a gunnery training vessel with an excellent antiaircraft battery, including two 1.1-inch quadruple, heavy machine-gun mounts.

Most of the cruisers and active destroyers in Pearl Harbor were modern, dating from the mid- to late 1930s. *New Orleans* (2–22) was one of the two heavy cruisers in the harbor on 7 December 1941. At that time she was moored to a pier in the Navy Yard's repair basin.

Completed in 1939, *St. Louis* (2–23) was one of the newest units in the Pacific Fleet. Her antiaircraft armament topped that of any other U.S. cruiser. It comprised four 1.1-inch quadruple mounts and four twin 5-inch, 38-caliber mounts fully enclosed in gun houses. In the summer of 1941 she had Measure 1 camouflage with a Measure 5 false bow wave painted on her hull; on 7 December 1941 she had Measure 11 overall sea blue paint.

Two ships of the old scout cruiser type were in Pearl Harbor on 7 December 1941. *Detroit* (2–24) and *Raleigh* were completed in 1922. Despite their age, these vessels could make 35 knots. During the attack, *Raleigh* sustained bomb and torpedo damage; *Detroit*, flagship of Rear Adm. Milo F. Draemel, commander of the Pacific Fleet destroyers, had a narrow escape from a torpedo.

2–19. *California* **(BB-44), moored to TenTen Pier in Pearl Harbor during August 1941.**

2–21. *Utah* **(AG-16) being painted into Measure 1 camouflage at Mare Island in August 1941.**

2–20. *Oklahoma* **(BB-37) at left and** *Nevada* **(BB-36) lie moored to the quays along Ford Island on 3 November 1941.**

2–22. *New Orleans* (**CA-32**).

2–23. *St. Louis* (**CL-49**) in the summer of 1941.

2–24. The light cruiser *Detroit* (**CL-8**).

2–25. *MacDonough* (DD-351), a Farragut class destroyer.

2–26. *Phelps* (DD-360), a Porter class destroyer.

2–27. *Conyngham* (DD-371), a Mahan class destroyer.

The most numerous type of vessel in Pearl Harbor when the Japanese struck was the destroyer. With four exceptions, none dated before 1934. They represented four classes: eight of the Farragut class (2–25), two Porters (2–26), eight Mahans (2–27), and eight Gridleys (2–28). These vessels reacted well during the attack and claimed several kills.

Many older flush-deck destroyers, most dating from the early 1920s, had been converted to minecraft in the 1930s. A number of them, including the destroyer-minelayer *Montgomery* (2–29), lay in Pearl Harbor on 7 December 1941.

Three flush-deckers of World War I vintage were still in service as destroyers and stationed at Pearl Harbor. All of them, including the *Chew* (2–30), were at moorings on that day. *Ward*, which was patrolling off the harbor entrance on 7 December 1941, fired the first American shots of the Pacific war. She sighted and sank a Japanese midget submarine more than an hour before the air attack began.

Most of the Pacific Fleet's submarines were out of Pearl Harbor, either at sea or in various ports, when the Japanese struck. Only four remained in slips at the submarine base or at TenTen Pier. *Dolphin* (2–31) was one of the former. She had portholes on the front of the conning tower that were somewhat reminiscent of Jules Verne's *Nautilus*.

2–28. *Ralph Talbot* (DD-390), a Gridley class destroyer.

2–31. *Dolphin* (SS-169).

2–29. *Montgomery* (DM-17) moored with three other minecraft in Pearl Harbor early in 1941.

2–30. Flush-deck destroyers *Chew* (DD-106), at left, and *Ward* (DD-139) at Hilo in July 1941.

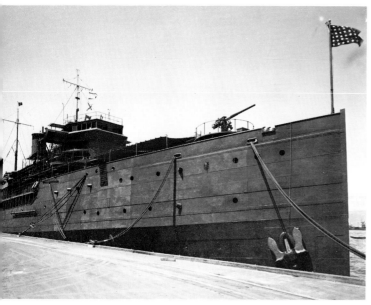

2–32. *Oglala* (CM-4).

2–33. The hospital ship *Solace* (AH-5).

2–34. The Curtiss P-40B.

One of the oldest ships in Pearl Harbor that December morning was the minelayer *Oglala* (2–32). Completed in 1907, she so seldom left the dock that once, according to Walter Lord, birds built a nest in her funnel. As the flagship of Minecraft, Battle Force, however, she had her own importance and seemed to have a likable personality.

One vessel in Pearl Harbor on 7 December 1941 had a unique mission. *Solace* (2–33), the only hospital ship in harbor, was solely concerned with treatment of the wounded. Busy with patients and with no way to fight back during the attack, her personnel could only hope that the Japanese would continue to ignore her. She received a Navy Unit Commendation for the crew's outstanding work on that day.

The ships of the Pacific Fleet were not charged with defending themselves in harbor. That job was the primary responsibility of the Army's Hawaiian Department and its air arm, the Hawaiian Air Force. A close second was its mission to protect the Hawaiian Islands from invasion. In both tasks, the Hawaiian Air Force (HAF) was to be the first line of defense that would sink or turn back the enemy before it could land. To that end, as of 7 December 1941, the United States had built up the HAF to an impressive 754 officers and 6,706 enlisted men. The organization was divided into two major components: the Eighteenth Bombardment Wing and the Fourteenth Pursuit Wing, headquartered respectively at Hickam and Wheeler fields. The

2–35. The Curtiss P-36A.

Eighty-Sixth Observation Squadron of the bombardment wing was stationed at Bellows Field, and one fighter squadron was training at little Haleiwa Field in northern Oahu.

The primary fighter aircraft on Oahu was the Curtiss P–40B/C (2–34), of which eighty-seven were assigned to Wheeler, counting those at Haleiwa. Only fifty-two of them were in commission. In addition, twelve were at Bellows, all operational. The P–40 was a current type that could be effective in the hands of a skilled pilot, but it was no match for the Zero. Still less competitive were the obsolescent P–36s (2–35), of which only twenty of the thirty-nine assigned were operational, and the P–26s. Fourteen of the latter type were on hand, ten in commission.

Most of Hickam Field's bombers were obsolescent Douglas B–18s, "Bolos" (2–36). The inventory showed thirty-two, but only twenty of these medium bombers were in commission. Even if airborne on 7 December 1941, they undoubtedly would have been sitting ducks for the Zeros. The Bolo was slow, carried a relatively small bomb load, and had weak defenses.

Vastly superior was the heavy bomber, the Boeing B–17—the legendary "Flying Fortress" (2–37). A pilot's dream machine, the B–17 inspired in its crews something of the love the sailors felt for their ships. On paper Hickam had twelve; in fact, only six were fit to fly.

The other bombers at Hickam were twelve light Douglas A–20As (2–38), five of them in commission.

2–36. The Douglas B-18 "Bolo."

2–37. The Boeing B-17D "Flying Fortress."

2–38. Douglas A-20A "Havoc."

2–39. The Grumman F4F-3 "Wildcat."

Most of the HAF's observation aircraft were assigned to the Eighty-Sixth Observation Squadron at Bellows. They included six O–47Bs, of which four were operational, and two O–49s, both in commission. A few aircraft of other types were stationed at Wheeler, including two A–12 light bombers.

Thus, when the Japanese struck, the HAF had on hand only sixty-three modern, operational combat aircraft—eleven bombers and fifty-two fighters—pathetically outnumbered by Japan's air armada. To make matters worse, Lieutenant General Short had ordered the aircraft lined up on the ramps for convenience in protecting against sabotage by the local Japanese, including Japanese-Americans, both of whom he firmly believed were Oahu's main danger.

Of course, the Navy was not subject to Short's directive, but results of the attack were quite as devastating as if it had been. At Ewa Marine Air Base, Fighter Squadron VMF-211 had eleven F4F–3 "Wildcats" (2–39) assigned, with all but one operational. The Wildcat was to perform well during the war, but on 7 December Japanese machine-gun fire destroyed nine of Ewa's eleven.

Ewa's offensive punch was divided between two types of scout bomber—twenty-four of the Douglas SBD "Dauntlesses" (2–40) and eight Vought SB2U "Vindicators" (2–41). What their operators thought of the Vindicator may

2–40. Douglas SBD-1 "Dauntless."

2–41. Vought SB2U-3 "Vindicator."

be deduced from the unofficial nicknames "Vibrators" and "Wind Indicators." The Dauntless proved itself over and over throughout the Pacific war, notably at Midway, but 7 December was not its day. The Japanese shot up eighteen scout bombers at Ewa. By 7 December, except for a few utility aircraft, the Marines' colorful aircraft paint jobs had yielded to an overall light gray.

Along with the Hawaiian Air Force's bombers, the Navy's Consolidated PBY "Catalinas" (2–42) formed the nucleus of long-range reconnaissance ability. Thirty-six, all but three of them operational, were assigned to Kaneohe Naval Air Station. Four of Ford Island Naval Air Station's thirty-five Catalinas were under repairs; another four were airborne. The Japanese inflicted devastating damage to this type of aircraft, twenty-seven of which were destroyed at Kaneohe and nineteen at Ford.

The OS2U–3 "Kingfisher" floatplanes (2–43) assigned to the battleships sustained heavy losses. Five of the ships had dispatched their complements to Ford Island, but nine Kingfishers remained aboard *West Virginia*, *Oklahoma*, and *California*. Only two of these survived the raid, and those sent to Ford Island also fared badly.

In addition to its combat aircraft, the Navy had on Oahu a number of small utility planes either lightly armed or unarmed. Two such were the Grumman J2F (2–44) and

2–43. An OS2U-3 "Kingfisher" alongside its ship, *Arizona*, during exercises on 6 September 1941.

2–42. Consolidated PBY-5 "Catalina."

2–44. Grumman J2F "Duck" from the Navy utility squadron VJ-1.

Sikorsky JRS–1 amphibians (2–45). These planes added color to the military scene, for they still retained their prewar finishes. For example, the JRS-1s were silver with chrome yellow wings and a willow green tail empennage. After the attack, these planes proved useful in aerial scouting near Oahu.

The Pacific Fleet's shipboard antiaircraft (AA) defense consisted of a variety of weapons. In late 1941, the battleships and most of the cruisers carried eight 5-inch, 25-caliber (here *caliber* is the length from breech to muzzle, divided by the diameter of the bore) AA guns in single open mounts (2–46). Except on the new light cruisers *Helena* and *St. Louis*, which shipped the newer 5-inch, 38-caliber mounts, no protective gun houses surrounded these mounts. During the attack, this shortcoming proved to be fatal, for many gun crewmen suffered casualties because of insufficient splinter protection.

The standard AA weapon aboard all the newer destroyers was the 5-inch, 38-caliber mount (2–47) in open, semi-enclosed, or enclosed configurations. On *St. Louis* and *Helena*, these guns were mounted in pairs and protected by large gun houses. Later, during wartime refits, many of the older cruisers and battleships replaced their 5-inch, 25-caliber mounts with the more effective 5-inch, 38-caliber twin mounts.

On some auxiliary vessels and on the old light cruisers *Raleigh* and *Detroit*, the primary AA defense was the 3-inch, 50-caliber gun (2–48). The Navy also employed them as interim mounts aboard carriers, battleships, and cruisers until the new 1.1-inch quadruple mount became available. Of World War I vintage, these guns possessed neither the range nor the destructive power of the 5-inchers.

Even less effective were the 3-inch, 23-caliber guns (2–49) employed on auxiliaries and older ships. With very limited range and accuracy, it was perhaps the most ineffectual weapon mounted in 1941.

At the beginning of the war, the Navy's principal medium-range AA weapon was the 1.1-inch quadruple, heavy machine-gun mount (2–50). Before the war, the King Board Program had called for four such mounts on each battleship and cruiser. However, manufacturing difficulties hampered the program, and only one of the battleships in Pearl Harbor, the *Maryland*, was so armed when the Japanese struck. Later the heavier Bofors 40-millimeter mounts replaced these weapons.

At the outbreak of the Pacific war, the close-range AA protection aboard the U.S. fighting ships was woefully inadequate. In this category, each of the Pacific Fleet's battleships and cruisers could muster only eight water-cooled, .50-caliber machine guns (2–51). As the ships came in for refits in late 1941 and early 1942, the Oerlikon 20-millimeter mount replaced most of the fleet's .50-caliber weapons.

2–45. A VJ-1 Sikorsky JRS-1 amphibian.

2–46. A 5-inch, 25-caliber AA mount.

2–47. A 5-inch, 38-caliber AA mount.

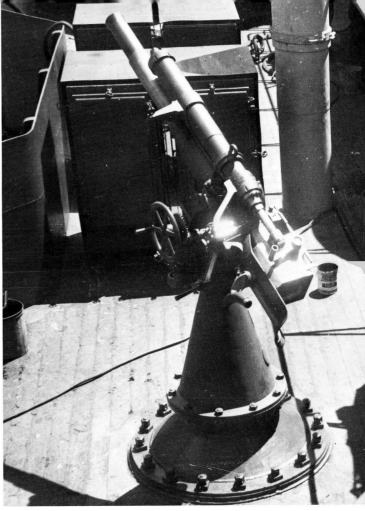

2–49. A 3-inch, 23-caliber AA mount.

2–48. A 3-inch, 50-caliber AA mount.

2–50. The 1.1-inch quadruple heavy machine-gun mount.

2–51. Browning water-cooled, .50-caliber machine gun.

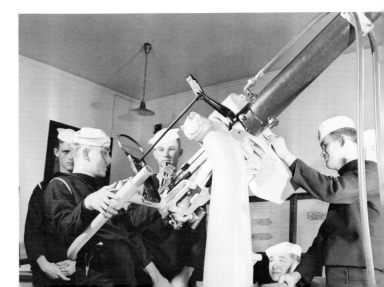

The Setting

Time does not stand still, even in Hawaii, and anyone visiting the islands for the first time since 1941 would find many almost stupefying changes. Up to World War II, Honolulu was still to a large extent the city encountered in the Charlie Chan mysteries—big enough to have all the modern conveniences but small enough for an easygoing, civilized life-style in a setting of unsurpassed beauty. On 7 December, a Japanese pilot noticed the sugarcane bending at his plane's approach; today the sugarcane plantations are gone, victims of urban sprawl. Yet some things never change—the matchless climate, the sea, the mountain peaks, and the gracious hospitality.

The military installations, too, have altered surprisingly little. The old hangar lines at the air bases still exist, and most of the landmarks in and around Pearl Harbor remain intact. In 1941, many of Pearl Harbor's facilities were new, dating from after August 1939. The installations included a completed battleship drydock and another under construction; an 18,000-ton floating drydock; a repair basin with industrial establishments capable of repairing any type of ship; a fuel depot with two tank farms; a submarine base; and a section base housing the inshore patrol and harbor entrance control post. Then, too, headquarters for the Pacific Fleet and the Fourteenth Naval District were located there.

Although popularly considered to be impregnable, Pearl Harbor had at least one major disadvantage of which the Navy was acutely aware. If a large ship should sink in the narrow channel, it would close the harbor for weeks, perhaps months, not only trapping any ship in harbor but also denying entrance to those outside (3–1). That is why, on 7 December, the Japanese swarmed down on *Nevada* when she attempted a sortie.

One stroke of luck for the Americans on 7 December was the fact that the Pearl Harbor attack plan contained no provision for destroying the Navy Yard (3–2). Had the Japanese done so, they would have put the U.S. Pacific Fleet out of action far more effectively than by wrecking individual ships. The fleet would have had no choice but to return to the Pacific Coast. This withdrawal could have significantly altered the course of the war. Instead, the Navy Yard was able to begin repairs almost as soon as the Japanese were out of sight and throughout the war to conduct business as usual, including the notable feat of repairing the *Yorktown*, badly damaged at the Coral Sea, in time to participate in the Battle of Midway.

One facility the Japanese did not overlook was Drydock No. 1 (3–3). Completed in 1919, the drydock had had an inauspicious beginning. According to local legend, its construction angered a resident shark god, who caused the walls to cave in. This setback appeased the god, who, after administering this slap on the wrist, permitted completion of the project. On 7 December the flagship *Pennsylvania* was in this drydock.

CHAPTER 3

3–1. Pearl Harbor on 31 October 1941 with Ford Island at the center, the Navy Yard, submarine base, and fuel oil tank farms at the left, and Hickam Field beyond the Navy Yard.

3–3. Drydock No. 1 and *Arizona* in 1932.

3–2. The Pearl Harbor Navy Yard on 13 October 1941.

Another Japanese error was in ignoring the submarine base in the southeast loch. As a result, the Pacific Fleet's submarines were able to operate effectively from the first. One reason for Japan's oversight may have been a misconception. Just as many Americans entertained the curious notion that Japanese could not make good fliers, many Japanese did not believe that Americans could become efficient submariners.

Probably the worst mistake the Japanese made was not including among their targets the Pacific Fleet's fuel supply, stored above ground in tank farms (3–4) near the submarine base. Destruction of these facilities would have crippled the entire Pacific Fleet because the Hawaiian Islands produced no oil; every pint had to be brought in by tanker and stored in the vulnerable tank farms. Their destruction would have rendered useless every military and naval installation in the islands. Fortunately for the Americans, the Japanese planners concentrated on the tactical tools of war—the ships and aircraft. In contrast, realization of the importance of the base facilities was one reason why many of Oahu's defenders, including Kimmel and Short, believed that the Japanese were more likely to attack when the fleet was at sea rather than in the harbor.

Back on *Akagi*, after the attack, Fuchida begged Nagumo to authorize a third major wave to kill off damaged ships and also to destroy logistical targets, but Nagumo decided upon immediate withdrawal.

Photograph **3–5** shows Ford Island from 9,800 feet, much the same view that Fuchida and his high-level bombers saw while making their runs on Battleship Row.

According to a crew member aboard *Argonne*, the best observation point during the attack was TenTen Pier (3–6), so called because it extended out 1,010 feet from the northern corner of the Navy Yard. *Pennsylvania* was customarily berthed there, but on 7 December she was in drydock.

The area surrounding Pearl Harbor was still largely undeveloped, so, except for the vicinity of the Navy Yard, the harbor had a tranquil, rural appearance (3–7 and 3–8). Yet in 1941, Oahu fairly bristled with military and naval installations, including a formidable assortment of airfields.

3–5. Ford Island on 10 November 1941 with Naval Air Station hangars at lower left.

3–4. Pearl Harbor's submarine base.

3–7. Pearl Harbor from *Argonne*'s bridge on 11 August 1941, showing *West Virginia*, *Arizona*, and *Oklahoma*.

3–6. *Pennsylvania*, flagship of the Pacific Fleet, lies moored to TenTen Pier on 11 August 1941, as seen from the *Argonne*.

Of these, the Hawaiian Air Force's Hickam Field (3–9) was the largest, with a complement of 4,894 enlisted men and 486 officers as of 30 November 1941. Located southeast of Pearl Harbor, Hickam was home to the Eighteenth Bombardment Wing. The commanding officer at Hickam Field was Col. William E. Farthing (3–10).

Hickam was one of the newest and most modern military bases on Oahu, with graceful palm trees lining a carefully planned system of streets and avenues. Its attractive Art Deco main gate glistened in the famed Hawaiian sunshine (3–11).

Wheeler Field, headquarters of the Fourteenth Pursuit Wing, was Oahu's primary fighter base, with a complement of 2,978 enlisted men and 279 officers as of 30 November 1941. Wheeler had been expanded in the late 1930s with much new construction. On 7 December 1941, its aircraft were parked in front of the hangar line (3–12). Wheeler's commanding officer was Col. William J. Flood (3–13).

3–9. Hickam Field in October 1941, with the Hale Makai Aircrew Barracks just behind the hangar line and Hawaiian Air Depot hangars at the bottom.

3–8. The light cruiser *St. Louis* (right) rests beside *Montgomery* (left) and *Breese* in the Navy Yard's Repair Basin in October 1941.

3–10. Col. William E. Farthing, commanding officer, Hickam Field.

3–12. Wheeler Field in October 1935.

3–13. Col. William J. Flood.

3–11. Hickam Field's main gate in the late 1930s.

The Noncommissioned Officers' Club (**3–14**) was typical of Wheeler's spruce, well-kept facilities. Such solid, polished, manicured installations as Wheeler created the impression of self-assured order and stability. In such surroundings, the idea of attack from without could have seemed unbelievable.

One of the Hawaiian Air Force's auxiliary landing strips, supplementing the main airfield at Wheeler, was Bellows Field, located on the eastern shore of Oahu (**3–15**). As of 30 November 1941, its complement was 350 enlisted men and 59 officers, mainly the Eighty-Sixth Observation Squadron. On 7 December the Forty-Fourth Pursuit Squadron was also at Bellows. Lt. Col. Leonard D. Weddington (**3–16**) was commanding officer at Bellows. His domain was quite a departure from Hickam and Wheeler. Accommodations were sparse, and the main gate (**3–17**) was a far cry from Hickam's Art Deco showpiece.

Bellows was palatial beside Haleiwa Field, which had no installations at all. Originally used as an emergency landing field, in 1941 it had only an unpaved landing strip (**3–18**), and it was in use to simulate real battle conditions for gunnery training. Those on temporary duty there had to bring their own tents and equipment. On 7 December, the Forty-Seventh Pursuit Squadron was at Haleiwa and there had its first taste of actual combat.

3–15. Bellows Field

3–14. Wheeler Field's Noncommissioned Officers' Club.

3–17. Bellows Field's main gate.

3–16. Lt. Col. Leonard D. Weddington.

3–18. Haleiwa Field on Oahu's northwest coast.

Kaneohe Bay Naval Air Station was one of Oahu's newer installations, still under construction on 7 December (3–19). Located on Oahu's eastern shore, Kaneohe was designed as a major seaplane base for PBY patrol bombers. In command at Kaneohe was Comdr. Harold M. ("Beauty") Martin, a popular and respected officer (3–20).

The Navy concentrated much of its long-range reconnaissance aircraft at the Pearl Harbor Naval Air Station on Ford Island (3–21). The seaplane ramp and hangars lay at the foot of the island. When aircraft carriers were in port, their air groups parked in front of the hangar line on Ford Island's west side. Capt. James H. Shoemaker (3–22), a hearty and energetic officer, was in command of the Pearl Harbor Naval Air Station.

3–20. Comdr. Harold M. ("Beauty") Martin.

3–19. Kaneohe Bay on 1 October 1941; note the unfinished hangar.

3–21. Pearl Harbor Naval Air Station, 10 October 1941, as Lt. Comdr. Kakuichi Takahashi saw it at 0755, 7 December 1941.

3–22. Capt. James H. Shoemaker.

The Marines on Oahu concentrated their aviation activities at Ewa Marine Corps Air Station (3–23) west of Pearl Harbor, under the command of Lt. Col. Claude A. Larkin (3–24). Few if any envied him the job, for Ewa was universally regarded as a sisal-choked, dusty backwater (3–25). Nevertheless, during all of 1941 it developed at a feverish pace to become the base for Marine Air Group Twenty-One. Personnel frequently referred to Ewa as the "Mooring Mast Field" because of its dirigible mast constructed during the 1930s. It survived into the 1940s as a control tower.

Wherever their duty stations, servicemen on Oahu headed for Honolulu whenever they could. Photograph 3–26 shows Honolulu Harbor and the surrounding city from the air. In 3–27, one of Honolulu's most readily recognizable landmarks, the Aloha Tower, forms part of the background for troops lining up by platoon in the park on Fort Street during 1940. In a March 1942 shot (3–28), a sailor steps out briskly at the corner of Fort and King streets, one block south of Hotel Street in downtown Honolulu.

3–25. Ewa's JRS-1 amphibian braves one of the many dust storms that plagued the base.

3–23. Ewa Marine Corps Air Station in October 1941.

3–24. Lt. Col. Claude A. Larkin.

3-26. The city of Honolulu and its harbor on 13 January 1941.

3-27. Left: Army troops form up behind the Aloha Tower.

3-28. Downtown Honolulu on 8 March 1942.

The Voyage to Hawaii

Between the large Japanese island of Hokkaido and the long, mountainous peninsula of Kamchatka lies a chain of islands stretching more than six hundred miles across the northern Pacific. The Russians call them the Kuriles ("smoking islands") because they are frequently veiled in heavy fog; the Japanese call them Chishima Retto ("thousand islands") because of their great number. The largest of the group is Etorofu. Roughly midway on its eastern side is fog-bound Hitokappu Bay, some six miles across and extending about the same distance inland. The Japanese settled upon it as the perfect rendezvous point. To maintain secrecy, Nagumo's vessels left their home ports and slipped into Hitokappu Bay over a period of several days.

We know of no official chart showing the anchorage plan; however, in 1943, the British interrogated a captive, Sea3c. Shigeki Yokota. He had been aboard *Kaga* during Operation Hawaii and from memory drew two maps of Hitokappu Bay with ship positions and features of the surrounding terrain (4–1).

As the units of the First Air Fleet rendezvoused in late November, Operation Hawaii was still on a need-to-know basis. The ships' crews and many of the officers had no idea of their ultimate destination as they arrived at Hitokappu Bay (4–2).

An extraordinary atmosphere of isolation and uncertainty was the temporary lot of the crewmen. Photo 4–3 shows the stark, barren landscape of Etorofu, as seen from *Zuikaku*'s flight deck. Note that a feeble attempt was made to fortify the island; ropes lashed to the upper works provided some scant additional protection to the bridge area (4–4).

The mountains surrounding Hitokappu Bay provided a desolate backdrop for *Akagi*, Nagumo's flagship (4–5). Fog

4–2. Hitokappu Bay, 22 November 1941, showing (left to right) *Kirishima,* **an oiler,** *Kaga,* **and** *Hiei.*

4–1. Anchorage plan of the Pearl Harbor Strike Force at Hitokappu Bay.

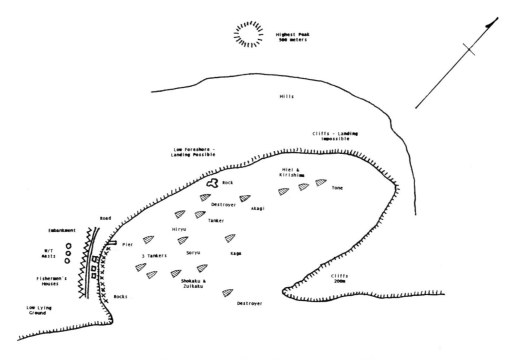

4–3. Hitokappu Bay seen from *Zuikaku*'s flight deck.

4–4. Crewmen cluster about *Zuikaku*'s wind-whipped forecastle on 26 November.

4–5. *Akagi,* flagship of the First Air Fleet, at Hitokappu Bay.

4–6. Aviators (foreground) and gun crews (right) bundled in heavy flight gear on *Akagi*. Other carriers lie in the misty background (from left to right): *Kaga, Shokaku, Zuikaku, Hiryu,* and *Soryu.*

4–7. *Kansen* AI-156 on board *Akagi*.

in the distance reinforces the eerie impression created by photo **4–6**, taken aboard *Akagi;* note dive-bombers spotted on deck at right.

Even at such a remote location as Hitokappu Bay, security had to be maintained. Aboard *Akagi*, Zero AI-156 in **4–7** was one of the ready aircraft. It carried no auxiliary fuel tank, the propeller had been pulled through the "prime" position, and the cockpit stood open, ready for the pilot to jump in and take off at a moment's notice.

What none of these topside pictures can convey is any hint of the urgent activity below decks. On 22 November, those in the know received a lengthy, important briefing from an officer who had been dispatched to Oahu to obtain information. The next morning, Nagumo took into his confidence all his commanding officers and staffs, although, of course, many already knew their destination. An all-morning tactical and operational meeting followed. That afternoon all the flying officers were told the secret, and the rest of the day was spent in detailed operational briefings

4—9. Attempts to provide extra protection to the _Akagi_.

4—8. The First Air Fleet under way at last from Hitokappu Bay.

with last-minute adjustments to the plan. This activity continued the next day, and then finally the crews received the news of their destination from their own officers.

Battle flags snapped in the knifing winds (**4–8**) as the sortie began early in the morning of 26 November (Japanese time). Once outside the harbor, the task force encountered heavy seas. For most of the voyage, however, the sea was unusually calm. Primary concern was not weather but security. Blackout prevailed at night and absolute radio silence at all times. Every possible protective measure was taken in case of discovery and attack by American ships or planes. Before the war, a common deficiency of many naval vessels, both Japanese and American, was insufficient splinter protection for the ships' exposed parts. In **4–9**, crewmen aboard _Akagi_ attempt to remedy the deficiency by tying rolled-up mattresses to the carrier's island superstructure. The quilted engine cover on the fighter is evidence that this photograph was taken while the task force was still in the northern latitudes.

Photo **4–10** shows gun crews standing alert on *Akagi*'s port antiaircraft gallery. Battle ensigns and signal flags snapped at the mainmast. Three Kates were standing by for action aboard *Akagi*, lined up behind a lone Zero. As seen from *Akagi*'s island in **4–11**, *Kaga* and *Zuikaku* steam in column on the horizon. Another shot of these two carriers shows them heaving in unison (**4–12**). Photo **4–13**, taken from *Akagi*'s stern, also shows *Kaga* and *Zuikaku* lumbering toward Hawaii under overcast skies.

Below decks, training, especially in recognition of U.S. warships, continued unabated. Officers primarily concerned with planning studied Operation Hawaii over and over, and no day went by without some adjustment. Senior officers never left the bridge unless absolutely necessary and slept in their uniforms.

One of their chief worries was refueling, without which the project would have been canceled or at least severely curtailed. Refueling was hazardous even under the best of conditions, and if the Pacific had acted up as it had on the sortie date the task force would have been in serious trouble. At that point, however, the sea had been so unusually calm that some considered it a special dispensation from heaven. In **4–14**, the tanker *Kenyo Maru* is shown approaching one of Nagumo's ships. But when launch time

4–11. Looking astern from the *Akagi*'s island, *Kaga* and *Zuikaku* steam on the horizon.

4–10. Gun crews at a twin 120-millimeter, 45-caliber AA mount on *Akagi*'s port gallery.

4–13. Another view of *Kaga* and *Zuikaku* headed for Hawaii.

4–12. *Kaga* and *Zuikaku* surge through the whitecapped swells.

4–14. *Kenyo Maru,* flagship of the First Supply Train tankers.

for the aircraft came, the sea was so rough that in training, or even a routine operation, flight operations would have been canceled. This picture (4–15) of a destroyer struggling through the heavy seas gives some idea of conditions.

Photo 4–16 shows an officer on *Shokaku*'s bridge addressing personnel on the flight deck below; 4–17 shows two lieutenant commanders holding a discussion, also on *Shokaku*'s bridge.

In the final hours before launch, excitement ran high,

fueled by such exhortations as that shown on the blackboard above Capt. Koji Shiroshima of *Shokaku*: "Japanese Imperial Fleet! You must obey and die for your country, Japan! Whether you win or lose, you must fight and die for your country!" (4–18). Another ship's blackboard bears two orders with a similar theme: "This is a crucial moment. The victory of the Emperor hinges on this battle. Exert [literally, smash] yourselves and make an extra effort for this battle" (4–19).

4–15. A destroyer from the Strike Force plunges through the northern Pacific.

4–16. Addressing men assembled on the flight deck from *Shokaku*'s bridge.

4-17. Officers talking on *Shokaku*'s bridge.

4-18. The presence of *Shokaku*'s skipper lends authority to the message on the blackboard above him.

4-17. Officers talking on *Shokaku*'s bridge.

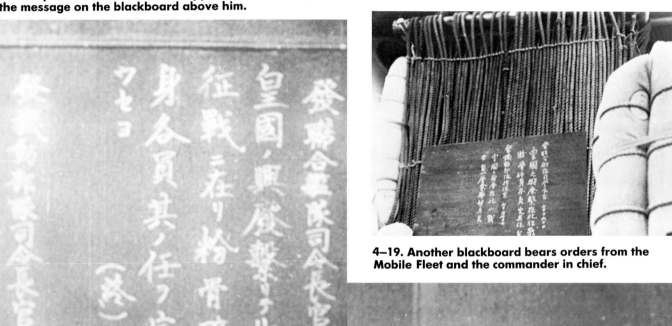

4-19. Another blackboard bears orders from the Mobile Fleet and the commander in chief.

4–20. Looking forward from *Zuikaku*'s island, *Kaga* steams on the horizon.

4–21. *Akagi* makes the final approach to Oahu.

As the task force steamed ever nearer to Hawaii, someone aboard *Zuikaku*'s island took this picture of *Kaga* as she was striving to keep the proper distance (4–20). The date then was 6 December 1941, and *Akagi* was making her final approach, accompanied by *Hiei* and *Kirishima* (4–21).

Aboard the flagship, officers briefed crew members from atop the island (4–22), and *Kaga*, too, was the scene of briefings (4–23). *Akagi* had taken special precautions, such as mounting a light machine gun on the superstructure (4–24).

Zuikaku's fighter pilots commemorated the occasion with one of the group photographs so dear to the Japanese of the time (4–25): At center, second row from the front, sat Lt. Masao Sato, the fighter unit leader (right), and Lt. Masatoshi Makino, Sato's second in command (left). The pair led a flight of five aircraft over Oahu the following day. Left of Makino was Lt. (jg) Yuzo Tsukamoto, who commanded the balance of *Zuikaku*'s fighter pilots in a combat air patrol over their fleet during the raid. Sporting a goatee at far right on the second row was P01c. Tetsuzo Iwamoto, who became the Imperial Navy's second-ranking ace, with eighty aerial victories. At the time, Iwamoto was already an accomplished ace with fourteen kills in China to his credit. Such wartime pictures, whether of friend or foe, are always poignant; they might well be the last. The *Zuikaku* was fortunate in that all her fighter pilots survived the engagement.

4–22. *Akagi* officers brief crew members on 6 December.

4–23. Lt. Ichiro Kitajima briefs *Kaga*'s aircrews on the torpedo attacks. Note the chalk-drawn map of Pearl Harbor.

4–24. Note the mattresses secured to *Akagi*'s island.

4–25. *Zuikaku*'s fighter pilots in a group portrait on 6 December.

The Flight to Oahu

The Pacific was still quite calm on 6 December when, from 0630 to 0830, the task force completed its final refueling. Exactly three hours later, the fleet reached an appointed spot and turned due south at an increased speed of 20 knots. Ten minutes later, to heartfelt cheers, *Akagi* hoisted the famous Z flag that Adm. Heihachiro Togo had flown at the battle of Tsushima in the Russo-Japanese War.

That night the airmen retired early to be fresh and alert for the ordeal ahead. While they slept, mechanics on the flight decks were tuning up the aircraft of the first wave, and in the hangars others made the second-wave planes ready. Last-minute intelligence had confirmed that much of the U.S. Pacific Fleet was in harbor and apparently unaware of danger. The weather, however, was becoming unfavorable. An overcast sky threatened visibility, and heavy seas pounding the vessels would make launching difficult and dangerous, with the carriers listing from 11° to 15°.

By 0530 the airmen had breakfasted and gathered in the briefing rooms of their respective carriers for final instructions and words of encouragement from ranking officers. At 0550 the carriers and their escorts headed into the wind for takeoff, which the weather delayed for twenty minutes. The months of meticulous planning and training were over; now success or failure was in the hands of Fuchida and his airmen. All the officers and crewmen who could be spared from their duties came topside to participate in the historic moment and to see their comrades off.

Unfortunately, no photographs are known to exist of the launching of the first wave in the dark. However, souvenirs of the second-wave takeoff convey the flavor of the whole.

With the first wave airborne, the task force once more turned south, while deck crews rushed to raise the aircraft of the second wave to the flight decks. Aboard *Akagi*, Lt. Saburo Shindo's *kansen* awaited the signal as ensigns and signal flags snapped to starboard in the brisk wind (5–1).

5–1. The Imperial Navy's air arm poised to launch behind Lt. Saburo Shindo's *kansen* on *Akagi*'s flight deck.

Shindo's wingman, PO1c. Tadao Kimura, was likewise ready, as *Akagi* turned into the wind (5–2). At last, Shindo's fighter lifted off, as *banzai* after *banzai* split the air (5–3).

Shindo was the first airman of the second wave aloft, but others soon followed (5–4). On *Shokaku*, Lt. (jg) Masao Iizuka, leader of the carrier's combat air patrol, revved up his plane (5–5). Once this patrol had taken off, plane

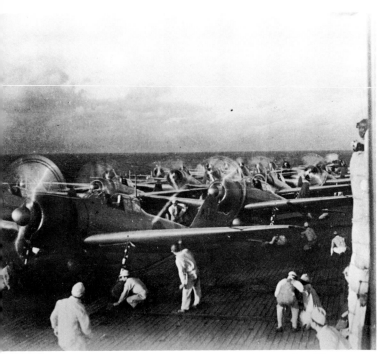

5–2. Lieutenant Shindo's wingman, PO1c. Tadao Kimura, prepared for takeoff at left in AI-101. Note the Type 99 carrier bombers further aft.

5–3. Lieutenant Shindo was the first airman from *Akagi*'s second wave to take to the skies.

5–4. On board *Akagi,* a Val lifts off in the early morning sunlight.

5–5. At right, Lt. (jg) Masao Iizuka revs up EI-104. Note the two wide, horizontal stripes of a *chutai-cho,* or division commander.

handlers spotted *Shokaku*'s other second-wave aircraft. In 5–6 they position a bomb-laden Kate. In 5–7 we see more activity aboard *Shokaku*, which had not been turned east into the wind. Twenty-seven Kates headed by Lt. Tatsuo Ichihara stood ready for takeoff (5–8).

At 0705 the carriers again increased speed and turned eastward into the wind. *Shokaku*'s air officer, Comdr. Tetsujiro Wada, lifted a white flag to signal takeoff (5–9), but the second wave remained poised briefly, delayed by the last aircraft of the carrier's air patrol. Upon releasing a fighter, deck crews crouched under its passing wings (5–10).

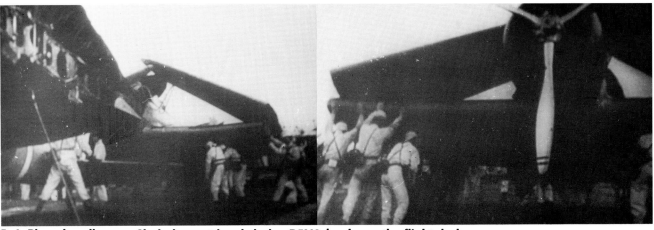

5–6. Plane handlers on *Shokaku* spot bomb-laden B5N2 *kanko* on the flight deck.

5–7. The Emperor's Sea Eagles rush to man *Shokaku*'s second-wave aircraft. Note the ship's bell in the background at left.

5–8. B5N2s prepared for takeoff. Two squadron-leader stripes distinguish Lieutenant Ichihara's aircraft.

5–9. *Shokaku*'s air officer signals takeoff.

5–10. The last fighter of *Shokaku*'s combat air patrol delays second-wave takeoff. Deck crews crouch under passing wings.

With bombs slung underneath, PO2c. Satoru Okimura's *kanko* lumbered down the deck to follow Ichihara, whose plane can be seen in the distance in the last photo. The crewmen in this shot wore a *hachimaki*. Such headbands usually bore a patriotic slogan such as "Certain Victory" (5–11 and 5–12). As a Kate leaped upward, men of the carrier shouted encouragement (5–13). Meanwhile, aboard the flagship *Akagi*, horizontal bombers of the second wave lifted off in the early morning sunlight. Originally the Japanese planned to take off at night and reach Oahu with the dawn. For safety considerations, however, this plan was retimed to take advantage of the light.

When all planes were launched, Nagumo turned his task force south once more until it reached a point approximately 180 miles off Oahu's northernmost point. The Japanese anticipated that many aircraft would be seriously damaged, so the mother ships were instructed to wait as near as possible to the scene of the attack. On the carriers' decks, crewmen continued to wave their caps as long as the planes were visible.

Photograph **5–14** shows one of the fifteen horizontal bombers from *Akagi* and its 800-kilogram, armor-piercing bomb, converted from a naval artillery projectile. Like Lt. Comdr. Shigeharu Murata's torpedomen, Fuchida's horizontal bombers were to have only one shot at the target.

Meanwhile the fates, as if reluctant to abandon the Americans entirely, gave them two opportunities to realize that something was sorely amiss and to go on the alert. The first chance came about through the midget submarine operation. These tiny craft were launched from standard submarines close to Hawaii. They were charged with entering the harbor and causing as much damage and confusion as possible. One did penetrate the harbor, where the destroyer *Monaghan* sank it. None did any damage, although Japanese propaganda lionized—almost canonized—the midget submariners to the extent of even crediting one with sinking *Arizona*.

5–11 and 5–12. Lieutenant Ichihara's wingman, PO2c. Satoru Okimura, pushes his throttle forward and follows Ichihara.

5–13. Men of the Fifth Carrier Division exhort their comrades in an outburst of patriotic emotion.

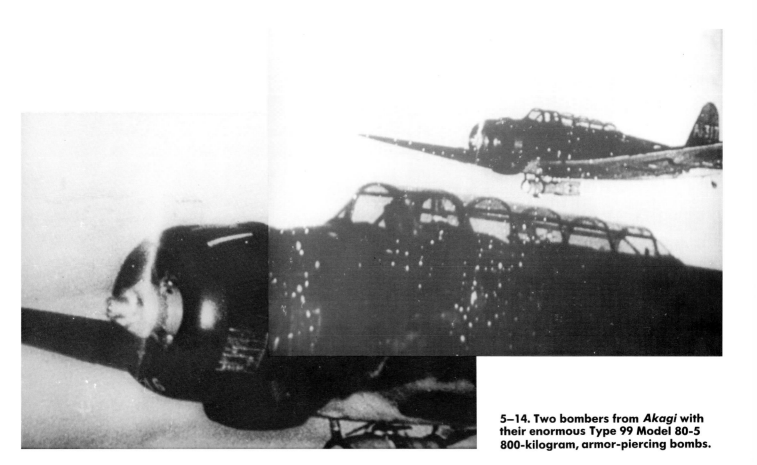

5–14. Two bombers from *Akagi* with their enormous Type 99 Model 80-5 800-kilogram, armor-piercing bombs.

A painting (**5–15**) based upon crewmen's service photographs was executed as a memorial. These crewmen (circling from left to right) are P02c. Yoshio Katayama, P01c. Naokichi Sasaki, P01c. Shigenori Yokoyama, Ens. Masaharu Yokoyama, Lt. Naoji Iwasa (leader of the group), Ens. Shigemi Furino, Ens. Akira Hiroo, P02c. Tei Ueda, and P02c. Kiyoshi Inagaki. Note that the artist showed all the petty officers as commissioned officers, probably to signify the posthumous double promotions all received. Conspicuous by his absence is Ens. Kazuo Sakamaki, who had the misfortune—from the Japanese standpoint—of being captured instead of killed.

Chart **5–16** shows the disposition of the midget submarines off Pearl Harbor.

While steaming south of Oahu on inshore patrol duty, the destroyer *Ward* (**5–17**) spotted one of the midget submarines off the entrance channel as it trailed the cargo ship *Antares* (**5–18**), a lighter in tow. Apparently the little craft's skipper hoped to enter the harbor entrance nets in concert with *Antares*.

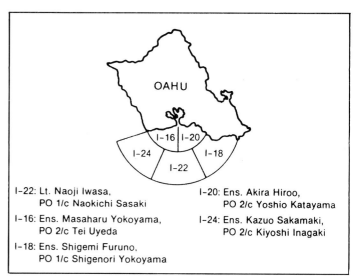

I-22: Lt. Naoji Iwasa,
     PO 1/c Naokichi Sasaki

I-16: Ens. Masaharu Yokoyama,
     PO 2/c Tei Uyeda

I-18: Ens. Shigemi Furuno,
     PO 1/c Shigenori Yokoyama

I-20: Ens. Akira Hiroo,
     PO 2/c Yoshio Katayama

I-24: Ens. Kazuo Sakamaki,
     PO 2/c Kiyoshi Inagaki

5–16. Arrangement of the five midget submarines.

5–15. The midget submarine crewmen of the Special Naval Attack Unit.

5–17. *Ward,* photographed 26 February 1919, painted in peacetime light gray.

5–18. *Antares,* during World War II.

At 0637 *Ward*'s officer of the deck, Lt. (jg) William O. ("Oscar") Goepner (5–19), summoned his skipper, Lt. William W. Outerbridge (5–20), who at 0640 ordered his destroyer to attack. At precisely 0645, 7 December 1941, the crew of *Ward*'s gun mount No. 3 (5–21) fired. The members of the gun crew are from left Gunner's Mate 3c. Edward J. Bukrey; GM3c. Joseph V. Fluegel; No. 3 Loader Sea1c. John A. Peick; No. 4 Loader Sea1c. Harold P. Flanagan; Gun Captain BM2c. Russell H. Knapp; No. 1 Loader Sea1c. Ambrose A. Domagall; Trainer Sea1c. Raymond B. Nolde; Sight Setter Coxswain Karl C. J. Lasch; and Pointer Sea2c. Clarence W. Fenton. The first shot missed, but the second scored a solid hit.

Thus the first shot of the attack on Oahu came from an American destroyer, not a Japanese aircraft. *Ward*'s track chart appears in 5–22.

5–21. The crew of *Ward*'s gun No. 3.

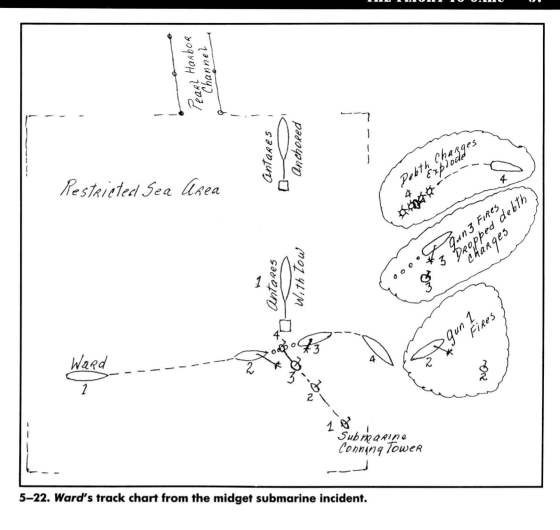

5–22. *Ward's* track chart from the midget submarine incident.

5–19. Lt. (jg) William O. Goepner.

5–20. Lt. William W. Outerbridge, circa 1942.

A U.S. plane, Catalina No. 14–P–1 (5–23), piloted by Ens. William P. Tanner (5–24), participated in this action. Tanner, copilot Ens. Robert B. Clark (5–25), and navigator Ens. Donald H. Butler (5–26) had taken off from Kaneohe on a routine antisubmarine patrol. Sighting what they thought to be an American submarine in difficulties, Tanner obligingly dropped two float lights. When, to their surprise, *Ward* attacked the submarine, Tanner and his colleagues joined in, dropping one of the PBY's depth charges. So both Patrol Wing Two and *Ward* claimed the sinking. Although the order in which the midget submarines met their deaths cannot be determined with certainty, the vessel's position suggests that this first submarine might well have been the craft manned by Ens. Akira Hiroo (5–27) and P02c. Yoshio Katayama (5–28).

5–23. Ens. William P. Tanner's PBY-5 14-P-1.

5–24. William P. Tanner as a captain in 1959.

5–25. Ens. Robert B. Clark, circa 1941.

5–26. Donald H. Butler as a commander in 1961.

5-27. Ens. Akira Hiroo.

5-28. PO2c. Yoshio Katayama.

The radio log of the section base at Bishop's Point (5–29) recorded *Ward*'s messages concerning the incident. Lt. Comdr. Harold Kaminski (5–30) was on duty at Fourteenth Naval District Headquarters and did his best to pass the information upward through channels. Yet so many false reports had been made of submarine contacts in the Oahu area that Admiral Kimmel was still awaiting confirmation of this incident when Fuchida's airmen struck.

If this first American opportunity strangled in red tape, the second was throttled by the proverbial long arm of coincidence. At the Opana Mobile Radar Station on Oahu's north coast, Pvt. Joseph Lockard (5–31) and Pvt. George Elliott were just about to shut down at 0700, their duty hours over. All at once their screen showed so unusual

a contact that they continued to trail it (5–32). First Elliott and then Lockard phoned the Fort Shafter Information. After some delay, Lockard spoke with Lt. Kermit A. Tyler (5–33), the pursuit officer on duty. Although Lockard described the blip as "the biggest sightings he had ever seen," the report rang no alarm bells in Tyler's mind. By a bitter coincidence, a flight of B–17s was due to land at Hickam Field that morning from Hamilton Field, California. They were indeed on the way, only some 5° off the Opana sighting. Assuming this to be what Opana had picked up, Tyler told Lockard, "Well, don't worry about it." As an exercise, and because they were interested, the two soldiers kept tracking the flight until they lost it at 0739.

```
                    R A D I O   L O G
                       SECTION BASE
                 BISHOP'S POINT, OAHU, T.H.
       WATCH                          RECEIVER &
                                      CONTROLS   O.K.
       G.E. GIBSON  SUPERVISOR
                                      FRE.  2670   KCS.  1941 R.W.H
       ROB. MOYLE   OPERATOR          DATE 7 DECEMBER 1942

  1715    TIME OF LAST ENTRY
  1721    DW2X  V  DN3L  AR
          DN3L  V  DW2X  K
          DW2X  V  DN3L  P BT WE HAVE DROPPED DEPTH CHARGES UPON SUBS
                        OPERATING IN DEFENSIVE SEA AREA AR
          DW2X  V  DN3L  STAND BY FOR MORE MESSAGES
          DNRL  V  DW2X  IMI YOUR LAST PRIORITY K
  1723    DW2X  V  DN3L  WE HAVE ATTACKED FIRED UPON AND DRIPPED DEPTH
                        CHARGES UPON SUBMARINE OPERATING IN DEFENSIVE SEA
                        AREA AR
          DW2X  V  DN3L  DID YOU GET THAT LAST MESSAGE K
          V  DW2X        R
          V  DN3L        STAND BY FOR FUTHER MESSAGES
```

5–29. *Ward's* radio messages.

5–30. Lt. Comdr. Harold Kaminski, watch officer in Rear Admiral Bloch's headquarters.

5–31. Pvt. Joseph Lockard in early 1942.

5–32. The *Opana* radar plot from 7 December 1941.

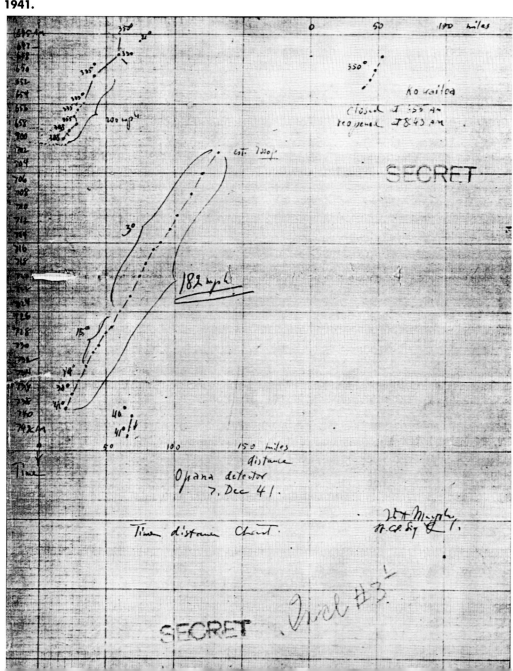

5–33. Lt. Kermit A. Tyler.

The First Wave

Attack on the Airfields

Exactly ten minutes after the Opana station lost track of the incoming Japanese flight, Fuchida gave the attack signal. Then at 0753, certain that he and his men had reached their goal without being discovered, he sent out the code "*Tora! Tora! Tora!*" to inform the Japanese Navy that the attackers had achieved surprise. In this case, according to plan, the slow, vulnerable torpedo planes would strike first before the Americans reacted and before smoke filled the sky. Misinterpreting the signals, however, Lt. Comdr. Kakuichi Takahashi, leader of *Shokaku*'s dive-bombing unit and overall commander of the first-wave dive-bombers, led his men into action first.

His airmen assaulted Hickam Field and the Pearl Harbor Naval Air Station at Ford Island. Nine of them, Takahashi in the lead, opened the raid by pounding the seaplane base at Ford Island. The lead plane succeeded only in churning up dirt and water on the ramp, but the rest of his group scored solid hits that turned Hangar 6 and the southern tip of Ford Island into an inferno of burning aircraft and a tower of smoke climbing skyward (6–1).

One of the first Americans to realize the significance of events was Rear Adm. William Rhea Furlong, commander, Minecraft, Battle Force (6–2). He saw Takahashi's missile strike and for an instant thought an American pilot had accidentally dropped his bomb. Then, spotting the red disk markings on the aircraft, he shouted, "Japanese! Man your stations!" and sent out the order, "All ships in harbor sortie!"

Standing at a window of the Ford Island command center, Lt. Comdr. Logan C. Ramsey (6–3) grasped the situation as the first bomb exploded. Racing to the center's radio room, he ordered the operators to broadcast in plain English, "Air raid Pearl Harbor. This is NOT [a] drill!"

Even as Takahashi's unit bombed Ford Island, the other eighteen dive-bombers under his command, among them Lt. Iwakichi Mifuku of *Shokaku* (6–4), were giving Hickam Field its first taste of war. Seen from a first-wave torpedo plane is the first stage of the assault on Hickam (6–5 and 6–6). Heavy smoke poured to the southwest from the hangar line and aircrew barracks; however, bombs had yet to fall among the B–17s and B–18s parked on the apron in front of the hangar line.

CHAPTER 6

6–1. Smoke boils up from the aircraft clustered around Hanger 6 on Ford Island.

6–2. Rear Adm. William Rhea Furlong.

6–3. Lt. Comdr. Logan C. Ramsey.

Dive-bombers

LTs. YAMAGUCHI & FUJITA

0755 9 PLANES

0755 9 PLANES

Fighters
0755 9 PLANES LCDR ITAYA

6–5. Diagram depicting the attack on Hickam Field.

6–6. The assault on Hickam Field begins.

6–4. Lt. (jg) Iwakichi Mifuku, leader, Twenty-Second Section, *Shokaku* dive-bombers.

After working in concert with *Kaga*'s fighters at Ewa, Lt. Comdr. Shigeru Itaya (**6–7**) and his airmen, including his second in command, Lt. (jg) Masanobu Ibusuki (**6–8**), proceeded to Hickam and took over where the dive-bombers left off. They strafed aircraft hangars and barracks and even chased individual servicemen down Hickam's broad avenues.

Dive-bombers from *Zuikaku* under Lt. Akira Sakamoto (**6–9**) and one of his division leaders, Lt. Tomatsu Ema (**6–10**), led the assault on Wheeler Field, while fighters from *Hiryu* under Lt. Kiyokima Okajima (**6–11**), as well as fighters from *Soryu*, established and maintained Japanese control of the airspace over Wheeler.

The 20/20 vision of hindsight recognizes the folly of concentrating so many aircraft so closely together (**6–12**). Pearl Harbor survivors often declare, "We got caught with our pants down." Few pictures more clearly illustrate the

6–7. Lt. Comdr. Shigeru Itaya, leader, first-wave fighter unit from *Akagi* and overall commander of the first-wave fighters.

6–8. Lt. (jg) Masanobu Ibusuki, shown here during 1945.

6–9. Lt. Akira Sakamoto, leader, *Zuikaku* dive-bombing unit.

6–10. Lt. Tomatsu Ema, one of Sakamoto's two division leaders.

6–11. Lt. Kiyokima Okajima, leader, *Hiryu* fighter unit of the first wave.

LT. SAKAMOTO
8802
25 PLANES

6–12. Diagram of attack on Wheeler Field.

pertinence of this phrase than this Japanese photo (6–13) showing Wheeler early in the raid. Any hope the Americans had of effectively repulsing the Japanese went up in flames along with the Eighteenth Pursuit Wing's aircraft. Note the plume of gray smoke rising from the Seventy-Fifth Service Squadron barracks at right center, immediately behind the hangar line.

In 6–14, Wheeler lies helpless before Sakamoto's dive-bombers from *Zuikaku.* No movement or activity among the Americans is visible. Ema found the "beautiful and quiet" sight that greeted them "almost fantastic." Two bombers at right pull out of their dives toward the north, while another *kanbaku* crosses in the opposite direction. Ironically, the initial Japanese success became a hindrance to them because towering columns of black smoke obscured many undamaged P–36As parked on the apron's west end.

The Marines fared no better. The nine Zeros from *Kaga* under the command of Lt. Yoshio Shiga (6–15), along with those from *Akagi,* immobilized Ewa MCAS with a devastatingly effective strafing. The base stretching out in the distance as seen from a First Carrier Division torpedo plane skirting Oahu's southern shore is shown in 6–16. This aircraft passed by Ewa just minutes before Shiga's fighters made their initial attacks on that installation.

Overcoming their initial shock, Ewa's Marines defended themselves as best they could (6–17), but small arms and light machine guns were no match for the firepower of the attacking fighters. Shiga particularly remembered a lone leatherneck returning the Japanese fire with a pistol and paid him "a good respect."

6–14. Wheeler Field under attack.

6–15. Lt. Yoshio Shiga, leader, first-wave fighters from *Kaga.*

6–13. Aircraft of the Eighteenth Pursuit Wing go up in flames.

6–17. Ewa Marines defend themselves with rifles.

6–16. Ewa Marine Air Corps Station, seen from a torpedo-laden *kanko* from *Kaga.*

No airfield on Oahu took a worse pounding than Kaneohe Naval Air Station, the relatively new installation located on Mokapu Peninsula. Lt. Tadashi Kaneko (6–18), leading *Shokaku*'s fighter unit, worked together with Lt. Masao Sato (6–19), heading *Zuikaku*'s fighter unit. Their combined aircraft reduced many of the base's PBY–5s to smoking wreckage. Following their attack, a PBY–5 of Patrol Wing One lay collapsed on the ramp at Kaneohe (6–20), while a blazing wing section was all that remained of another PBY–5 (6–21).

6–18. Lt. Tadashi Kaneko, leader, *Shokaku* fighter unit.

6–19. Lt. Masao Sato, leader, *Zuikaku* fighter unit.

6–20. A PBY-5 from VP-14 at NAS Kaneohe Bay.

6–21. The remains of a PBY-5 at Kaneohe, set afire by incendiary ammunition.

The Torpedo Attack

At the head of the task force's torpedo aircraft flew Lt. Comdr. Shigeharu Murata (6–22), the acknowledged torpedo ace of the Japanese Navy. His crews from *Akagi* attacked Battleship Row, as did *Kaga*'s torpedo bombing unit under Lt. Kazuyoshi Kitajima (6–23). Lt. Tsuyoshi Nagai (6–24) led *Soryu*'s torpedo bombers against the ships moored along TenTen Pier and those moored northwest of Ford Island. Meanwhile Lt. Heita Matsumura (6–25) of *Hiryu* led his torpedomen against Battleship Row and the vessels at TenTen Pier.

The next three photos provide a view of the unfolding torpedo attacks as seen from a Kate of the First Carrier Division, probably from *Kaga*. With Oahu's mountainous terrain passing below, three *kanko* near their objective (6–26). Flying parallel to Oahu's southern shore, the torpedo bombers approach the Pearl Harbor entrance channel. Note the smoke from Hickam Field in the distance (6–27).

6–22. Lt. Comdr. Shigeharu Murata, leader, *Akagi* torpedo bombing unit, and overall leader of the torpedo attack.

6–23. Lt. Kazuyoshi Kitajima, leader, *Kaga* torpedo bombing unit.

6–24. Lt. Tsuyoshi Nagai, leader, *Soryu* torpedo bombing unit.

6–25. Lt. Heita Matsumura, leader, *Hiryu* torpedo bombing unit.

6–26. Three *kanko* lumber around the western side of Oahu toward their objective in Pearl Harbor.

6–27. Torpedo bombers nearing the Pearl Harbor entrance channel.

Two *Akagi kanko* accomplished their mission as two torpedo geysers rose alongside *Oklahoma* and *West Virginia* (6–28). The sight of these columns of dirty water brought relief from tension and anxiety to the handpicked torpedomen. One after another exclaimed exultantly, "*Atarimashita!*" (It struck!)

"General Quarters" (6–29) sounded on ship after ship moored along Ford Island as they sustained blows from both the northwest and the southeast. A *kanko* from *Soryu* pulled up steeply over the island after attacking *Utah* on the northwest side (6–30). The Japanese did not intend to waste precious torpedos on the old target ship, but an eager young lieutenant thought he saw Nagai attack her and did likewise, much to Matsumura's disgust. Its missile discharged,

6–28. Two *Akagi kanko* meet with success.

6–29. The bugle call "General Quarters."

GENERAL QUARTERS

Sounded as a signal for every man to go to his station for general quarters.

6–30. A view from southwest of Ford Island shows ships moored along Ford Island sustaining blows from both the northwest and southeast.

the aircraft banked and turned south, in accordance with the ruse to convince the Americans that the task force was south of Oahu. At right can be seen another *kanko* banking steeply over NAS Pearl Harbor and a water geyser erupting high into the air above *Oklahoma*. Note the PBYs near the hangars at the southern end of Pearl Harbor.

Often published, **6–31** reveals the vulnerability of the Pacific Fleet at Pearl Harbor: Lined up like "ducks in a shooting gallery," the battleships were perfect targets. Four splashes document how closely the Japanese approached the ships before releasing their torpedoes. Two wakes lead directly to *West Virginia*, where a geyser erupts from the water alongside the ship. Torpedo wakes also streak toward *Oklahoma* and *California*. The latter has just sustained its

6–31. Battleships lined up like "ducks in a shooting gallery."

first torpedo hit, which times this photo as slightly after 0800. In the far distance, smoke pours from the hangar line at Hickam. One of the nine dive-bombers under Takahashi pulls out over the harbor after bombing Ford Island. The attack cost the Japanese five torpedo bombers, among them that of Lt. Mimori Suzuki (6–32).

At 0805, after two torpedo hits, the target ship *Utah* strained against her mooring lines with a 30° list (6–33). Her crew did not have time to finish raising the flag at her stern. With her torpedo blisters removed, *Utah* had little chance of surviving the torpedo attack. She capsized at 0810, to reveal the torpedoed light cruiser *Raleigh* ahead (6–34). The layer of heavy timber came loose, tumbled into the water, fouled the channel and the waters surrounding *Utah*'s berth, and interfered with the crew's attempts to abandon ship.

During the raid, many heroic deeds passed unnoticed and unmentioned in official reports. Of those recognized, none is more compelling than that of Chief Watertender Peter Tomich of *Utah* (6–35). As her list increased and water surged through the vessel, many were trapped below decks. To ensure the escape of his men, Tomich stayed behind at his station in the pumping room and thus sealed his own doom. The Navy awarded him the Medal of Honor posthumously.

Accounts of individual resourcefulness and bold action abound. As an example, Lt. Claude V. Ricketts (6–36), on his own initiative and with the permission of his mortally wounded skipper, commenced and directed counter-flooding activities aboard *West Virginia*. A boatswain's mate and two shipfitters assisted in his efforts, which doubtless saved the ship from capsizing.

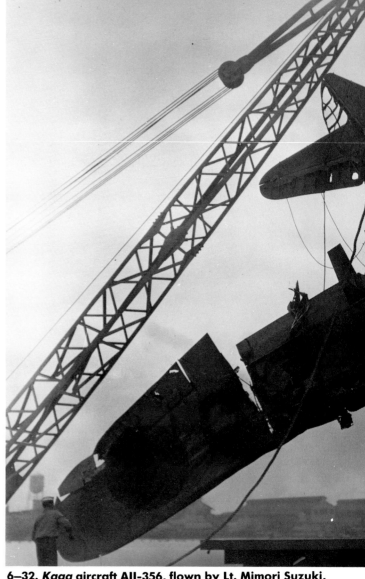

6–32. *Kaga* aircraft AII-356, flown by Lt. Mimori Suzuki, pulled from the waters of the southeast loch.

6–33. *Utah* listing after two torpedo hits.

6–35. Medal of Honor winner Chief Watertender Peter Tomich of *Utah*.

6–36. Lt. Claude V. Ricketts, shown here after the war.

6–34. *Utah* capsizing at 0810.

The Horizontal Bombing Attack

Pictured next are leaders of the four first-wave, high-level bombing units: Comdr. Mitsuo Fuchida, *Akagi* (6–37); Lt. Hideo Maki, leader of *Kaga*'s second group (6–38); Lt. Heijiro Abe, *Soryu* (6–39); and Lt. Comdr. Tadashi Kusumi, *Hiryu* (6–40).

At 0800, forty-nine horizontal bombers under Fuchida's overall command began their attack runs on Battleship Row from the southwest. This Japanese photo (6–41) shows the battleships as seen by Fuchida and his men ten thousand feet above the harbor. *Oklahoma* and *West Virginia* list heavily to port. As the lists increased, their OS2U–3 float-planes toppled into the water. A torpedo explosion ripped *Oklahoma*'s port side, *West Virginia*'s port side was awash, and fuel oil hemorrhaged from both ships. One bomber formation—probably the five *kanko* under *Kaga*'s Lt. Hideo Maki—had just bombed *Arizona* and *Vestal* in this photo and scored hits on *Vestal* and on *Arizona*'s No. 4 turret. Fragments and splinters splash around the battleship's fantail. A Japanese airman took this photo shortly before the explosion of *Arizona*'s forward magazines.

Photograph 6–42 shows *Arizona* shortly before her explosion. *Nevada*'s bow is at left, and *West Virginia* heels 25° to port. Then a bomb exploded in *Arizona*'s forecastle and detonated her forward magazines. That explosion, shown in 6–43 taken by an American, was the most stunning moment of the raid. The fact that any American photographer could capture this event on film is extraordinary in itself.

6–37. Comdr. Mitsuo Fuchida, leader, *Akagi* horizontal bombing unit.

6–38. Lt. Hideo Maki, leader, Second Chutai, *Kaga* horizontal bombing unit.

6–39. Lt. Heijiro Abe, leader, *Soryu* horizontal bombing unit.

6–40. Lt. Comdr. Tadashi Kusumi, leader, *Hiryu* horizontal bombing unit.

6–41. The battleships as seen by Fuchida and his men 10,000 feet above the harbor.

6–42. *Arizona* shortly before her explosion.

6–43. A bomb exploding in *Arizona*'s forecastle detonates her forward magazines.

6–44. Consumed in the conflagration, _Arizona_ lies at the north end of Battleship Row.

6–45. A clock recovered from _Arizona_.

6–46. Damage to the center-line gun of _Tennessee_'s No. 2 turret.

The Japanese credited their crack bombardier, PO Noboru Kanai of _Soryu,_ with the devastating direct hit. As the colossal force of the explosion forced tons of air through the ruptured fireroom intakes, a plume of black smoke jetted out of _Arizona_'s funnel (**6–44**). This smoke may have given rise to the popular notion that a bomb went down _Arizona_'s funnel and caused the explosion. A clock recovered from the battleship displays a moment seared into American memories (**6–45**).

Squadron after squadron of Fuchida's horizontal bombers passed over Battleship Row and rained down their 16-inch, armor-piercing projectiles. Except for the strike on _Arizona,_ the bombs that scored hits did surprisingly little damage. However, shrapnel from a bomb explosion on _Tennessee_'s No. 2 turret (**6–46**) flew over to _West Virginia_ alongside, mortally wounding the latter's skipper, Capt. Mervyn S. Bennion, as he directed his ship's defense (**6–47**).

6–47. Shrapnel mortally wounded *West Virginia* skipper Capt. Mervyn S. Bennion.

6–48. Mess Attendant 2c. Doris Miller waits to receive the Navy Cross.

6–49. Horizontal bombers from *Kaga* fly toward the rendezvous area. Antiaircraft fire spots the sky over the harbor. Note smoke from Hickam Field and Battleship Row.

One of those coming to Bennion's aid was twenty-two-year-old Mess Attendant 2c. Doris Miller, *West Virginia*'s heavyweight boxing champion. Due to torpedo damage, Miller could not stay at his battle station in the AA magazines. He assisted in moving the wounded until ordered to the bridge to help care for his skipper. After Bennion died, Miller manned a machine gun on the conning tower near the bridge. For his heroism, Miller became the first black man to be awarded the Navy Cross. At a ceremony aboard *Enterprise* on 27 May 1942, Miller stands at far right (6–48), ready to accept the award from Adm. Chester W. Nimitz.

Their bombing runs complete, *Kaga*'s high-level bombers began the return flight to their carrier, turning toward the rendezvous area west of Oahu. The Navy's tank farms were untouched by the raiders (6–49).

6–50. Smoke obscures battleships forward of *Arizona*.

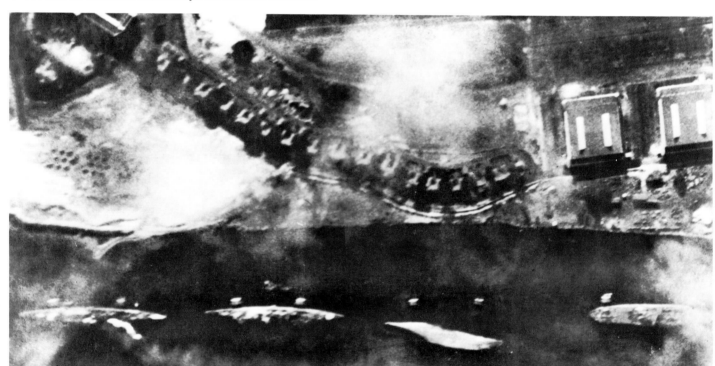

6–51. Ships on the northwest side of Ford Island between 0820 and 0840. *Utah* (left) has turned turtle while *Raleigh* lists discernibly to port.

6–52. Battleship Row.

The First Wave Continues

Following *Arizona*'s explosion, thick smoke obscured the four battleships forward of her. In **6–50**, taken from above Battleship Row between 0820 and 0840, *Oklahoma* (right) has capsized, rolling far out to port, and *Nevada*'s main battery is trained to starboard (left), probably to correct a list to port after sustaining torpedo damage. At the opposite side of Ford Island, *Utah* (left) has "turned turtle" in her berth. Left of *Utah*, *Raleigh* lists discernibly to port. Note the aircraft hangars at upper right in **6–51**.

Among the first American still photographs taken during the attack is **6–52**. On the north end of Battleship Row, *Nevada* (right) is shown still resting at her mooring. *Vestal* lies alongside *Arizona*, the latter burning furiously after her magazine explosion. Next in line are *West Virginia* and *Tennessee*. Ricketts's counterflooding efforts appear to have begun, for *West Virginia*'s list seems less pronounced. At far left, beside *Maryland*, *Oklahoma* lies capsized, although not yet fully settled in the harbor mud. By late in the attack, only the red of her underside was visible above water. Several factors—the presence of *Nevada* and *Vestal* and the condition of *West Virginia* and *Oklahoma*—establish the time of this photograph as approximately 0820 to 0825.

Primary concerns aboard *Arizona* quickly became fire fighting and removal of the wounded. The senior surviving officer, Lt. Comdr. Samuel Glenn Fuqua (**6–53**) provided invaluable leadership. After the ship blew up, he led the fire fighting on the quarterdeck and supervised evacuation of the wounded. When *Arizona* finally became untenable, he ordered all hands to abandon ship. For his heroism and devotion to duty, Fuqua received the Medal of Honor.

A half-dozen sailors stand in and around a small boat on *Tennessee*'s starboard bow in photo **6–54**. Smoke from *Arizona* has blocked most of the sunlight from the southeast, hence the dark, murky setting. The center barrel of the No. 2 turret is depressed slightly as a result of a hit from one of Fuchida's horizontal bombers. Note the enormous hawsers securing *Tennessee* to the concrete mooring quay at left.

6–54. Damage from bomb splinters scars the area surrounding the *Tennessee*'s conning tower.

6–53. Lt. Comdr. Samuel Glenn Fuqua of *Arizona*.

6–55. *California* holds her own at about 0830.

6–56. Beyond *California*, Old Glory still waves.

6–57. Battleship Row behind the smoke. The seaplane tender *Avocet* in the foreground was one of the first ships to fire on the torpedo planes.

Signal flags fluttering, *California* heeled to port, having taken two torpedo hits. Astern of her, the oiler *Neosho* shows no evidence of casting off her lines from the gasoline wharf, setting the time of photo **6–55** at about 0830. Behind her, smoke rises from Battleship Row and obscures the harbor to the north. Beyond *California*, oily smoke from the battered vessels forms a blackened, greasy backdrop for the Stars and Stripes, still flying on Ford Island despite the destruction (**6–56**). On the shore of Ford Island farther south, Battleship Row disappeared completely behind a pall of smoke. Note the large number of vehicles parked on Ford Island near the building at left in **6–57**.

The B–17 Flight

Around 0810, a flight of eleven B–17s—the same that Tyler assumed to be the Opana sighting—arrived over Oahu in the thick of the first-wave attack. Originating at Hamilton Field, California, the flight consisted of the Thirty-Eighth Reconnaissance Squadron (one B–17E and four B–17Cs) under Maj. Truman H. Landon (**6–58**) and the Eighty-Eighth Reconnaissance Squadron (six B–17Es) commanded by Maj. Richard H. Carmichael (**6–59**).

Photograph **6–60** reveals a B–17 under Japanese attack. Carrying no ammunition and only skeleton crews, the Flying Fortresses were totally defenseless. Several sustained damage and casualties from both enemy and friendly fire during their crews' frantic efforts to land at various airfields on Oahu. Understandably enough, many American defenders mistook the B–17s for Japanese and blazed away at them. Among the Japanese who attacked the B–17s was Lt. Shoichi Ogawa of *Kaga* (**6–61**), during the second wave.

6–58. Maj. Truman H. Landon in 1943.

6–60. A B-17 from the West Coast flight comes under attack.

6–59. Maj. Richard H. Carmichael in 1942.

6–61. Lt. Shoichi Ogawa, leader of the Second Chutai of *Kaga's* second-wave dive-bombers.

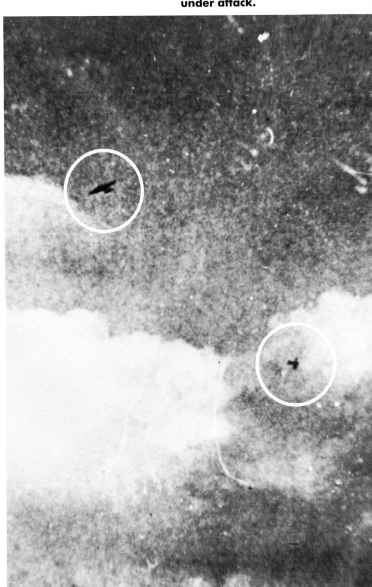

6–62. Bombers near one of the Hamilton Field, California, B-17s.

6–64. S. Sgt. Lee Embree.

6–66. Carmichael's wingman, Lt. Harold N. Chaffin.

6–63. Lt. Karl Barthelmess.

6–67. Lt. Bruce G. Allen.

6–68. Pilot Raymond T. Swenson.

6–70. Copilot Earnest I. Reid.

From the B–17s' vantage point, little evidence of an air raid was visible, apart from the smoke rising from Ford Island, and the B–17 crews did not immediately recognize that an attack was under way. Some thought a drill was in progress or perhaps some sort of celebration. Landon at first assumed that the aircraft flying toward him were a Hawaiian Air Force welcoming escort. These illusions rapidly dissolved as the Japanese opened fire. Two dive-bombers hovered near the B–17 (6–62) piloted by Lt. Karl Barthelmess (6–63). One of his crewmen, S. Sgt. Lee Embree (6–64), who took the photograph of the bombers, said that the aircraft veered away when he pointed his camera at them.

As the big bombers sped about in search of a place to put down, a chief petty officer at Pearl Harbor thought, Jesus Christ, the Japanese are really coming in now! And an experienced B–17 pilot at Hickam asked himself, Where did the Japs get four-engine bombers? Thus the defenseless B–17 crews had to contend with American as well as Japanese attacks.

In the view from the harbor in 6–65, looking northeast past *Avocet*, a B–17 pilot, possibly Carmichael or his wingman, Lt. Harold N. Chaffin (6–66), despairs of landing at Hickam and heads for Haleiwa with landing gear down.

Landon made it to Hickam, as did Lt. Bruce G. Allen (6–67). Capt. Raymond T. Swenson (6–68) landed his B–17C at Hickam while under attack by three of Itaya's fliers. They ignited flares in the bomber's radio compartment; the plane burned in half as it skidded down the runway (6–69). Itaya himself claimed credit for this B–17 kill, the first in the Pacific war, although he mistook the plane for a transport. The B–17 crew escaped except for Lt. William R. Schick, a flight surgeon, gunned down while running for safety. Out of habit, copilot Lt. Earnest I. Reid (6–70) set the parking brakes before bolting from the flaming wreck. Barthelmess also landed safely at Hickam. In 6–71 his crew checks over their gear.

6–65. A B-17E heads northwest toward Haleiwa Field.

6–69. Capt. Raymond Swenson's B-17C. Itaya claimed credit for its destruction.

6–71. Lieutenant Barthelmess's crew after landing at Hickam Field. One of Hickam's B-17Ds that escaped the morning attacks sits in the background.

Hickam's ground gunners exacted payment from this section of Itaya's fighters. As they swooped over Swenson's B–17C, machine-gun fire from among the Fifty-Eighth Bombardment Squadron's A–20s, parked near Hangar 2, struck aircraft AI–154. Its pilot was Itaya's wingman, PO1c. Takashi Hirano. His Zero fell into nearby Fort Kamehameha, where it careened into the ordnance machine shop (6–72).

Meanwhile, with three wounded crewmen aboard and unable to land at Hickam, Lt. Robert H. Richards (6–73) was forced down and landed his B–17C wheels up at Bellows Field on Oahu's east side (6–74).

6–73. Lt. Robert H. Richards.

6–72. *Kansen* AI-154 flown by PO1c. Takeshi Hirano of *Akagi*.

6–74. B-17C at Bellows Field, piloted by Lt. Robert H. Richards.

SBD *Flight from* Enterprise

A little after 0600, the carrier *Enterprise*, returning from an aircraft-ferrying mission to Wake Island, launched a routine patrol of eighteen SBD Dauntless scout bombers, which was a normal action. To maintain radio silence, Admiral Halsey did not inform Pearl Harbor of the flight. So when he received word of the attack, his first reaction was, "My God, they're shooting at my own boys!"

Leader of the SBD flight was Lt. Comdr. Howard L. Young (6–75). With him in his aircraft (6–76) was Lt. Comdr. Bromfield B. Nichol, Halsey's assistant operations officer. Seeing the AA bursts as they neared their destination, Nichol said to himself, My God, the Army has gone crazy, having antiaircraft drills on Sunday morning! Dodging Japanese aircraft and American AA, Young managed to land at Ford Island.

Lt. Masaji Suganami (6–77) led a first-wave unit of eight fighters from *Soryu*. They claimed five aerial kills during dogfights with the SBDs. Although preoccupied with their strikes on Ewa, Shiga's fighters also engaged the SBDs. They tangled with Ens. John Vogt (6–78) and Radioman (RM) Third Class Sidney Pierce (6–79). Some

6–75. Lt. Comdr. Howard L. Young (right) with VS-6 skipper Lt. Comdr. Hallsted L. Hopping in late 1941.

6–76. SBD-2 (BuNo 2162), the aircraft Young flew into Oahu on 7 December.

6–77. Lt. Masaji Suganami, leader, first-wave fighter unit from *Soryu*.

6–78. Ens. John H. L. Vogt.

6–79. RM3c. Sidney Pierce.

observers claimed that these Americans were engaged in a twisting dogfight almost at ground level when they collided with an attacking Japanese plane. Their aircraft (6–80) crashed near Ewa, and its wreckage intermingled with that of the Japanese fighter. Neither American survived the crash.

Lt. Clarence E. Dickinson (6–81) and RM1c. William C. Miller (6–82) fell victim to Suganami's fighters. Dickinson bailed out at very low altitude and survived, but Miller perished in the aircraft, which crashed near Ewa Beach (6–83). Ens. John R. ("Bud") McCarthy (6–84) and RM3c. Mitchell Cohn (6–85) likewise fell near Ewa (6–86). McCarthy bailed out and broke his leg, but Cohn could not free himself and was killed.

Lt. (jg) Frank A. Patriarca (6–87) tried to return to *Enterprise* but had to set down at tiny Burns Field on Kauai (6–88). His wingman, Ens. Walter M. Willis (6–89), as well as Coxswain Fred J. Ducolon, perished when their aircraft crashed into the sea off Oahu's southern coast, vic-

6–83. SBD-3 (BuNo 4570) flown by Dickinson and Miller.

6–80. Ensign Vogt's SBD-2 (BuNo 2160) lies in the brush near Ewa.

6–82. RM1c. William C. Miller.

6–81. Lt. Clarence E. Dickinson.

6–84. Ens. John R. McCarthy.

6–85. RM3c. Mitchell Cohn.

6–87. Lt. (jg) Frank A. Patriarca.

6–89. Ens. Walter M. Willis.

6–86. McCarthy and Cohn's SBD-2 (BuNo 2158). The card attached to the wreckage reads, "NAVY CRASH 7 DEC. 1941 INVESTIGATION COMPLETED. DO NOT REMOVE THIS SIGN."

6–88. Burns Field on 26 August 1941.

tims of Japanese fighter planes. Dive-bombers from *Shokaku* shot down Ens. Manuel Gonzales (**6–90**) and RM3c. Leonard J. Kozelek (shown with his shipmate RM3c. Audrey Coslett, **6–91**) some ten miles west of Oahu. No trace of the two fliers was ever found. American AA fire shot down Ens. Edward T. Deacon (**6–92**) and Coslett. They tried to reach Hickam's runway but fell short and landed in several feet of water in the Pearl Harbor entrance channel. Although both men were wounded, Deacon pulled Coslett into their life raft and paddled to an Army rescue boat that came out to meet them.

Quite by coincidence, Staff Sergeant Embree's busy camera caught the crash site of one of the *Enterprise* SBDs (probably Vogt's or Dickinson's) just north of Ewa Beach (**6–93**). A column of smoke marks the impact, while two Japanese aircraft circle about south of the crash.

Eventually, all the SBDs that landed safely made their way to Ford Island's Naval Air Station, some landing during the morning, others returning by way of Ewa MCAS. In what became a nerve-wracking game of runway hopscotch, seven of the SBDs landed at Ewa toward the end of the raid, but edgy ground crews told them to leave. The seven aircraft took off and attempted to land at Ford Island. Three made it successfully, but AA fire was so heavy that four pilots elected to return to Ewa. This time the Marines were more hospitable, servicing and arming the Navy's scout bombers. The last *Enterprise* aviator to depart Ewa was Ens. Carlton T. ("Misty") Fogg (**6–94**). In **6–95**, Ewa's ground crews service his SBD.

6–90. Ens. Manuel Gonzales.

6–92. Ens. Edward T. Deacon, on board *Enterprise*, January 1942.

6–91. RM3c. Leonard J. Kozelek and his shipmate RM3c. Audrey G. Coslett.

6–93. SBD crash site.

In the meantime, startled citizens of Honolulu looked upward, wondering what was causing all the noise and smoke (6–96). Many needed some time to realize that this activity was not just another, unusually realistic U.S. exercise. Soon defective American AA shells began tumbling into downtown Honolulu. The explosion and resulting fires caused a number of casualties and substantial property damage.

6–94. Ens. Carlton T. ("Misty") Fogg, circa 24 January 1942. Fogg would be dead within a week, shot down in the Marshalls.

6–95. Ground crews at Ewa service and arm Ens. Carlton Fogg's SBD, aircraft 6-S-11.

6–96. Honolulu residents look toward Pearl Harbor.

6–98. Comdr. John S. Phillips.

6–101. Lt. Comdr. William P. Burford in 1953.

6–97. Pearl Harbor from the north at about 0830.

6–99. *Neosho* pulls clear of the gasoline wharf at Ford Island shortly after 0842.

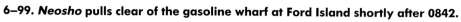

Pearl Harbor During the Lull

At about 0830, a brief lull between the two attack waves gave the harried Americans a chance to catch their breaths. In **6–97**, taken from the hills north of the harbor, AA fire has ceased, for no flak bursts spot the sky. No fires yet burn in the drydocks, although smoke is discernible at left over Hickam. Note the pall of smoke covering Ford Island and Battleship Row.

Comdr. John S. Phillips (**6–98**), skipper of the oiler *Neosho*, decided that things were getting too hot at the gasoline wharf in the middle of Battleship Row. At 0835 he ordered the tanker to back away from the wharf. Accordingly, she cast off her mooring lines and began backing away at 0842. In **6–99**, *Neosho*, just visible behind *California*, has pulled clear of the gasoline wharf. Note the

personnel in skivvies preparing to disembark onto the boat landing in **6–100**. However much these men may have wanted to put up a fight, this photo reinforces the overall impression of American unpreparedness.

At least one of the Japanese midget submarines eluded American patrols and successfully navigated the treacherous approach to Pearl Harbor's entrance channel. Before the submarine could reach its objective, it had to pass one last barrier—an antisubmarine net suspended from a boom, or gate, across Pearl Harbor's entrance channel. However, the gate was left open for nearly four hours, permitting the small boat to enter the harbor sometime between 0500 and 0800.

After penetrating the harbor, the midget submarine attempted to circle clockwise around the northwest side of Ford Island. There it ran afoul of the destroyer *Monaghan*, commanded by Lt. Comdr. William P. Burford (**6–101**).

6–100. Men disembarking on the southern end of Ford Island. Note *Neosho* at right.

6–102. *Monaghan* at Mare Island on 17 February 1942.

6–104. The midget submarine rammed by *Monaghan.* Depth-charge detonations produced the washboard effect on the submarine's hull.

6–106. Ens. Kazuo Sakamaki.

6–107. PO2c. Kiyoshi Inagaki.

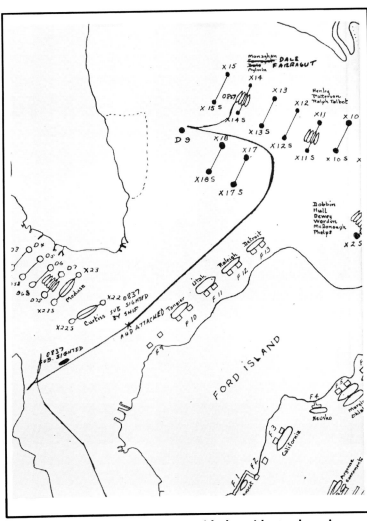

6–103. *Monaghan*'s engagement with the midget submarine.

6–105. *Curtiss* scored a direct hit on the midget at 0840.

Monaghan (**6–102**) was the first destroyer to get under way after the attack began. At 0837, when she was abreast of No. 7 buoy, lookouts sighted a submarine 1,200 yards distant, some 200 to 300 yards off *Curtiss*'s starboard quarter. Burford ordered his crew to attack, and the destroyer leaped forward. A torpedo from the midget submarine passed close to *Monaghan*'s starboard side. Undeterred, the destroyer opened fire, depth-charged, rammed, and sank the intruder at 0844. *Monaghan* ran aground but regained the channel and stood out of the harbor at 0905. *Monaghan*'s track chart shows her movement during this engagement (**6–103**).

The midget submarine had sustained heavy damage during the encounter (**6–104**). The collision with *Monaghan* tore away the minisub's bow. Several other vessels also fired frantically at this target, including *Curtiss*, which claimed to have scored a direct hit on the conning tower at 0840 (**6–105**). The 5-inch projectile passed through the submarine without exploding.

The midget submarine crewed by Ens. Kazuo Sakamaki (**6–106**) and PO2c. Kiyoshi Inagaki (**6–107**) experienced

6–108. The midget submarine commanded by Ens. Kazuo Sakamaki at Bellows.

a number of mishaps and ended up beached off Bellows Field (**6–108**). Both men dived overboard, but Inagaki drowned. Sakamaki reached shore to attain the unenviable distinction of America's number one Japanese prisoner.

At least one midget submarine was still at large late on the night of 7 December. At 2241, the little craft crewed by Lt. (jg) Masaharu Yokoyama (**6–109**) and PO2c. Tei Ueda (**6–110**) sent a message to its mother submarine, *I–16*: "Successful surprise attack."

6–109. Lt. (jg) Masaharu Yokoyama.

6–110. PO2c. Tei Ueda.

Airfields During the Lull

Between the first and second waves, personnel at Kaneohe tried to regroup and salvage what they could after the early morning strafing attack. Near Hangar 1 in photo **6–111**, a car speeds down an avenue beside the hangar line, while a burning PBY–5 in the background spews a fountain of smoke and flare into the air.

6–111. Looking west toward Hangar 1, NAS Kaneohe Bay.

The situation near the fire area at Hangar 1 grew progressively worse during the lull. The destruction of Kaneohe's only fire truck in the first attack on the base hampered fire-fighting efforts considerably (**6–112**). Photo **6–113** shows a score of bluejackets pulling a partially burned PBY–5 clear from the center of the fire area at Hangar 1. Note the fabric burned away from the aircraft's control surfaces.

A similar salvage effort was under way south on the seaplane ramp at the water's edge, although the PBY–5 was somewhat the worse for wear, with its wing burned off outboard of the port engine. In photo **6–114**, two officers and four enlisted men pull on a line only recently secured to the PBY's empennage by a sailor, who is just visible in the water under the starboard horizontal stabilizer. Fire-fighting foam covers the ramp, as a small dog—perhaps a mascot—at the water's edge takes in the scene.

Ground personnel at Ewa dispersed their aircraft throughout the lull in the fighting. Apparently their attempts were successful, as Marine records show that several aircraft survived the raid. Photo **6–115** shows an F4F–3 from VMF–211 upended on Ewa's apron at left, while one of VMSB–231's Vindicators is ablaze at center.

6–113. Fire fighters at work in front of Kaneohe's Hangar 1.

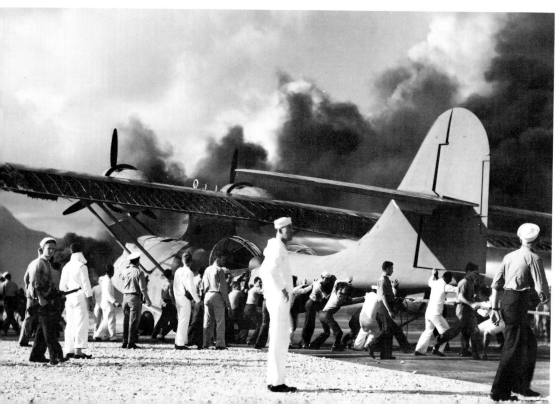

6–112. The fire area at Hangar 1.

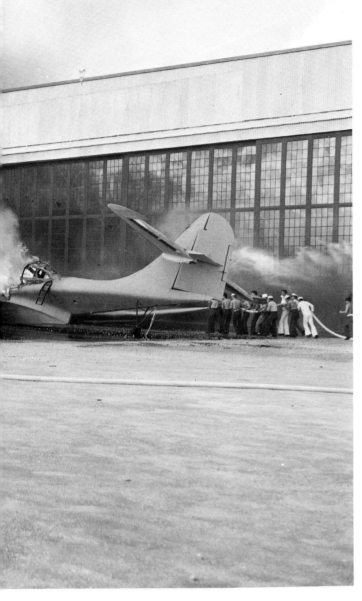

6–115. Ground personnel at Ewa rescue an aircraft.

6–114. Salvage efforts at Kaneohe.

The Second Wave

Hovering high above the scene of action, Fuchida heard the heavy drone as the second wave of aircraft approached the target, and his radio picked up Lt. Comdr. Shigekazu Shimazaki's "*To, to, to!*" The time was precisely 0854.

The Japanese planners knew that, with surprise no longer a factor, the slow, low-flying torpedo bombers would be so vulnerable that losses would outweigh results. Therefore, all the Kates devoted themselves to high-level bombing of the airfields. Lt. Comdr. Takeshige Egusa's dive-bombers had no preassigned targets; they were to destroy those ships the first wave had left operational. Thus action would depend upon judgment and visibility, and the dense smoke filling the sky over Pearl Harbor made the second quite difficult.

Lt. Takehiko Chihaya radioed *Akagi*, "Enemy defensive fire strong," but it was disappointingly ineffective from the American standpoint. Of the twenty Japanese aircraft (six fighters, fourteen dive-bombers) lost in the second wave, at least half fell to the few fighter pilots of the Hawaiian Air Force who managed to get airborne.

Nevada's *Sortie Attempt*

The single event during the attack that most attracted photographers was *Nevada*'s gallant effort to sortie from Pearl Harbor. The sight of this ship emerging from the shambles of Battleship Row and proudly standing down the channel stirred the hearts of thousands. *Nevada* and her brave crew provided a much-needed psychological lift for the Americans.

By 0830, Lt. Comdr. Francis J. Thomas, *Nevada*'s acting commander during the attack (**7–1**), knew that his ship was in a precarious position on the north end of Battleship Row. Already seriously damaged, *Nevada* remained an inviting target, and the enormous fires consuming *Arizona* in the berth ahead threatened her no less than did Japanese aircraft. So Thomas decided that it was "urgently necessary to get under way to avoid destruction of the ship." The decision made, Chief Boatswain Edwin J. Hill (**7–2**) led his line-handling details to the mooring quays and, under fire, cast off *Nevada*'s lines, allowing her to drift away. Hill jumped into the water and swam back to his ship. Later, during the height of the dive-bombing attack, he disappeared in one of the blasts while he was attempting to let go the anchors on the bow. Hill became one of fourteen Medal of Honor winners at Pearl Harbor.

At the end of the lull, *Nevada* backed unassisted out of her berth at about 0840, as *Arizona* burned out of control, her oil fires engulfing *Tennessee*. *West Virginia* listed to port but was still free of the large fires that broke out around her foremast later in the attack. Swinging clear of *Arizona*,

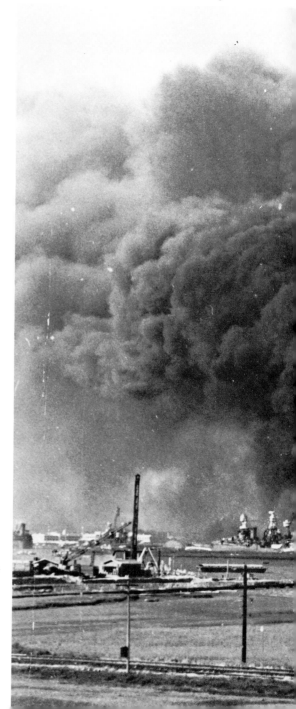

CHAPTER 7

7–3. *Nevada* **moves down Battleship Row.**

Nevada moved down the channel past Battleship Row. The heat was so intense that *Nevada*'s gunmen, turning their backs, clutched shells close to their bodies lest they explode.

Once past *Arizona*, *Nevada* picked up momentum, as thousands of anxious Americans watched (7–3). *Neosho*, having backed completely clear of her berth at the gasoline wharf, prepared to enter the Navy Yard. With no yardcraft lending assistance, *Nevada* successfully negotiated the channel beside Battleship Row. From a navigation standpoint, the most dangerous part of her attempt was still ahead, where the channel narrowed at the Navy Yard. In 7–4, *Nevada* can be seen moving down channel, as *California*, damaged by two torpedoes, heels over to port. After

7–1. Lt. Comdr. Francis J. Thomas.

7–2. Chief Boatswain Edwin J. Hill.

7–4. *Nevada* (right) continues down the channel beside Battleship Row.

7–5. Looking toward the Navy Yard from parking lot.

7–6. Seen from Ford Island's water tower, *Nevada* passes TenTen Pier at 0900. The seaplane tender *Avocet* is at lower right.

taking the previous photo, the photographer wheeled to his right and released his shutter just as flak bursts blossomed in midair to greet the Japanese second attack wave (**7–5**). Inboard TenTen Pier, *Argonne* nestled below the hammer-head crane in the Navy Yard next to *Oglala*, which was pulled astern of *Helena* at 0850.

As seen in **7–6** from Ford Island's water tower at the midpoint of her sortie, *Nevada* glided past TenTen Pier at 0900. At that instant, aircraft from *Kaga* commenced attacking *Nevada* from the south. Lt. Saburo Makino, leader of *Kaga's* dive-bombers (**7–7**), seized the opportunity to close the harbor by sinking *Nevada* in the entrance channel. The battleship's damage report demonstrates how Makino's dive-bombers executed their attacks (**7–8**). Although *Nevada's* track chart shows dive-bombing attacks occurring from the beginning of the sortie, the assault actually commenced when *Nevada* pulled abreast of TenTen Pier. As borne out by this chart and the photography that follows, the Japanese appear to have split up to attack *Nevada* downwind from the southwest and crosswind from the southeast. In all likelihood, Makino employed these tactics to split the American AA fire.

As *Kaga's* *kanbaku* mounted their dive-bombing assault, *Nevada* commenced burning from bomb hits forward. In **7–9**, *kanbaku* plummet down from the southwest in a de-

7–7. Lt. Saburo Makino.

7–8. *Nevada's* war damage. The chart confirms that only the aircraft attacking out of the sun scored hits.

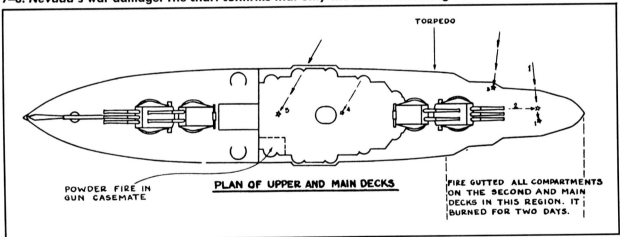

TORPEDO

POWDER FIRE IN
GUN CASEMATE

PLAN OF UPPER AND MAIN DECKS

FIRE GUTTED ALL COMPARTMENTS
ON THE SECOND AND MAIN
DECKS IN THIS REGION. IT
BURNED FOR TWO DAYS.

7–9. *Kaga's* dive-bombers assault *Nevada*.

termined effort to sink *Nevada* in the entrance channel. A third aircraft can be seen crossing from east to west. As the battleship pressed on, weathering a storm of bombs, yet another plane pulled out of its dive over the slow-moving vessel (**7–10**). Fires aboard *Nevada* (**7–11**) intensified as *Shaw* and the floating drydock came under attack from the three *kanbaku* of *Akagi*'s Twenty-Second Chutai, led by Lt. Shohei Yamada. Photo **7–12** shows a water geyser on *Nevada*'s bow and fires breaking out amidships following bomb hits on her boat deck and superstructure.

7–11. Fires on board *Nevada* (left) burn fiercely as a dive-bomber pulls out to the west to escape AA fire (far right) and a bomb detonates in the floating drydock (center right).

7–10. *Nevada* presses on, despite attacks from plane after plane.

7–12. A near miss on _Nevada_'s starboard bow veils the ship from view.

7–13. *Nevada* prepares to run aground.

7–14. *Nevada* (center) noses onto Hospital Point. Note *Argonne* at far left.

Down by the bow and burning forward and amidships, *Nevada* prepared to run aground at Hospital Point to avoid being sunk in the harbor channel. A collapsing water geyser from a near miss temporarily cleared fire and smoke from *Nevada*'s bow (**7–13**). Photo **7–14**, taken from a launch in the harbor between Battleship Row and the Navy Yard, shows *Nevada* nosing onto Hospital Point as *Shaw* burns furiously in the Floating Drydock, *Argonne* lies moored just inboard TenTen Pier, and smoke rolls skyward from *Cassin* and *Downes* in Drydock No. 1. A cameraman peering over *Avocet* from the roof of the headquarters building on Ford Island recorded the dramatic conclusion to *Nevada*'s sortie. In **7–15** she runs aground at 0910 as fires consume the forward part of the ship. Then Pearl Harbor's strong outbound current caught *Nevada*'s free-floating stern and pulled her out into the channel as her national ensign still flew defiantly from her fantail (**7–16**). After *Nevada* swung

7–15. *Nevada* runs aground.

7–16. The harbor's current pulls *Nevada* into the channel.

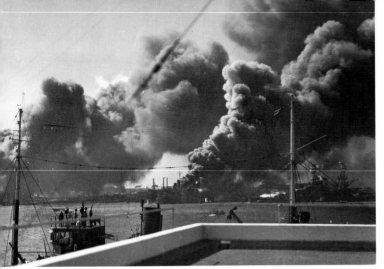

7–17. *Nevada* swings around, revealing *Shaw* at center.

completely around, *Shaw* is revealed at center in **7–17**, and the harbor tug *YT–153* is just visible alongside *Nevada* amidships. Ordered to help the battleship out of her berth at Ford Island, the tug found *Nevada* moving forward on her own. The little craft trailed behind *Nevada* throughout the sortie and thus was first on the scene when the battleship ran aground. *Pennsylvania*, having already weathered a hail of Japanese bombs, rests helplessly in Drydock No. 1 (**7–18**). Smoke from a bomb hit amidships at 0906 drifts away to the southwest. A large explosion ripped the destroyers *Cassin* and *Downes*, and *Neosho* headed for the Navy Yard, passing *California* shortly after 0900 (**7–19**).

7–18. *Pennsylvania* in Drydock No. 1.

7–19. *Neosho* stands down the channel.

Attacks Northwest of Ford Island

According to available records, Lt. Takehiko Chihaya's unit (7–20) attacked the vessels moored northwest of Ford Island simultaneously with Makino's attack on *Nevada*. This previously unpublished set of photographs (7–21 through 7–24) documents the dive-bombing attack of *Akagi*'s Twenty-Third Chutai (pilots PO2c. Yoshikazu Ota, PO3c. Kanesuke Homma, and Sea1c. Shuji Shimakura). In 7–21 flak bursts blossom above *Solace*, while two aircraft circle at low altitude opposite Ford Island; a *kanbaku* from *Akagi*'s Twenty-Third Chutai dives on *Curtiss*, moored west of Ford Island. In 7–22 an explosion erupts at 0905 as this dive-bomber, stricken and out of control, plunges into *Cur-*

7–20. Lt. Takehiko Chihaya, leader, *Akagi* dive-bombers.

7–21. *Akagi* bombers strike ships moored northwest of Ford Island. Note *Nevada*'s empty berth at left. A *kanbaku* diving on *Curtiss* is circled at upper left.

7–22. An *Akagi* bomber crashes on *Curtiss*.

7–23. Smoke marks the impact point on *Curtiss.*

7–24. *Curtiss* burning. Note *Medusa* at right.

tiss. These views are among the few American photos from the raid that show a Japanese aircraft attacking a specific, identifiable target. In **7–23** (looking west from *Tangier*), black smoke mushrooms from the impact point on *Curtiss*, which burns furiously following the collision. A few minutes later, at 0912, the ship sustained a bomb hit on the boat deck (**7–24**). The bomb passed through three decks, exploded on the main deck, and caused considerable blast and fire damage. A 250-kilogram bomb missed *Tangier's* port quarters by about twenty feet (**7–25**); shattered windows on her bridge attest to her narrow escape (**7–26**).

7–25. A bomb just misses *Tangier*.

7–26. *Tangier's* bridge.

Shaw *Explosion*

Following *Nevada*'s aborted sortie, *Shaw* continued to burn, attracting the attention of many observers, including several photographers (**7–27**). Fires spreading forward through the destroyer detonated *Shaw*'s forward magazines at 0930. In **7–28**, the initial fireball of the explosion mushrooms out of the stricken vessel. Tons of erupting high explosives heaved the fireball still farther into the air (**7–29**). The force of the explosion threw debris hundreds of feet away.

Flames enveloped *Shaw* and her drydock (**7–30**). The contrast of the brilliant fireball against the backdrop of oily smoke emanating from Drydock No. 1 heightened the drama and intensity of the scene.

7–27. *Shaw* continues to burn. Note *Nevada*'s bow afire (right).

7–28. Fires detonate *Shaw*'s forward magazines.

7–30. Flames cover *Shaw* in one of the most spectacular combat photographs of all time. Note *Nevada*'s silhouetted main battery (right).

7–29. Debris flies away from the shattered destroyer. Note garbage lighter *YG-21* at left.

Antiaircraft Fire and Aircraft

Photo **7–31** (looking from the heights beyond Pearl Harbor's north shore) shows a barrage of AA fire meeting the second wave. The Japanese arriving over the harbor encountered fully alerted vessels, but heavy smoke obscured the views and hampered the efforts of both attackers and defenders. Despite the impressive barrage, impromptu American gun crews, faulty ammunition, and cramped conditions in the moorings made American AA fire largely ineffective.

A Navy photographer caught a *kanbaku* at the moment of release toward a target somewhere in Pearl Harbor (**7–32**). In **7–33** a *kanbaku* with extended dive brakes and an empty bomb crutch is shown pulling up over the harbor. Personnel on Ford Island belted machine-gun ammunition during the attack. Most seemed absorbed in their task, but **7–34** shows a few wary upward glances as well there might be, with the presence of low-flying aircraft providing a constant reminder of danger. In **7–35**, a *kanbaku* skims only a few hundred feet above Ford Island. Another from either *Kaga* or *Hiryu* swooped down even lower, a scant hundred yards from a Navy photographer, who took the closest photograph (**7–36**) of a Japanese aircraft during the attack known to the authors.

7–32. A *kanbaku* releases its bomb.

7–31. Second-wave attackers encounter heavy AA fire.

7–33. A *kanbaku* pulls up over the harbor.

7–35. A *kanbaku* flies low above Ford Island.

7–34. Men on Ford Island belt machine-gun ammunition.

7–36. Another dive-bomber dips even lower.

Japanese reports indicate that Lt. Yasushi Nikaido, leader of the *Kaga* second-wave fighters, was responsible for maintaining control of the airspace over Pearl Harbor. One of his fighters banks steeply to the right during a low pass over Pearl Harbor (7–37).

A cluster of flak bursts over Army housing northeast of Hickam, close to Pearl Harbor (7–38). However reassuring this sight might have been to the Americans, the shrapnel from these explosions had to come down somewhere and did—quite often in populated areas around the harbor. Extensive civilian damage and many injuries, especially in Honolulu, resulted from American AA fire.

A section of dive-bombers maneuvers through flak bursts near the control tower on Ford Island (7–39). In 7–40, a dive-bomber goes down, its starboard gasoline tanks afire. In 7–41, a *kansen* meets a similar fate, and a thin plume of smoke or gasoline trails behind it. The Japanese lost twenty aircraft from the second wave, at least half destroyed by Army fighter pilots. The low number (seven or eight) legitimately claimed by AA fire over the harbor indicates the difficulties the American gun crews faced.

7–37. A fighter banks steeply over Pearl Harbor.

7–38. Flak over Army housing near Hickam Field.

7–39. Aichi Type 99 bombers near Ford Island's control tower.

7–40. A dive-bomber is shot down.

7–41. A damaged second-wave fighter over Pearl Harbor.

Attacks on the Navy Yard

Three aircraft appear over the Navy Yard and encounter only light AA fire (**7–42**). *Neosho* turned to port and headed up the southeast loch toward the temporary sanctuary of the Navy Yard. At 0903, Chihaya and the Twenty-First Chutai from *Akagi* attacked *Neosho* while she was en route. All three bombs missed, although "several bombs fell close to the stern, jarring the ship appreciably," according to *Neosho's* skipper, Commander Phillips.

Lt. Comdr. Takeshige Egusa, leader, *Soryu* dive-bombing unit, was overall leader of the second-wave dive-bombers (**7–43**). Some of his aircraft from *Soryu*, along with several from *Hiryu*, singled out the Navy Yard, among other targets, for punishment. Egusa personally opened the attack on *New Orleans*, one of the ships moored in the repair basin. Although his bomb missed, as did those of the other pilots, flying fragments blew twenty-seven holes in the ship, ranging from one to six inches in diameter. *New Orleans* was undergoing overhaul. During the raid, yard power to the ship failed. As the crew struggled to serve the 5-inch AA battery by hand, chaplain Lt. Howell M. Forgy (**7–44**) exhorted them to make the best of the situation and to "praise the Lord and pass the ammunition"—thus providing inspiration for one of the war's most popular songs.

Because American photographers concentrated on the area of greatest damage, few photographs exist of the Navy Yard during the raid. The following photos show the Navy Yard from the perspective of looking southwest from Pearl Harbor's submarine base at about 0915. In **7–45**, the submarine *Narwahl* and her crew fight back during the second wave, her union jack flying proudly from her bow. Black paint can be seen flaking and peeling at her hull; the ship's log mentioned the poor quality of the paint. The photo also shows *Honolulu*, *St. Louis*, *San Francisco*, and *New Orleans* moored in the Navy Yard's repair basin in the distance, as well as a large hammerhead crane over the oiler *Ramapo*, which is loaded with four motor torpedo boats forward of the funnel. In **7–46**, enemy aircraft catch the attention of the two sailors, now with rifles poised, and *Dolphin*, smallest of the Pacific Fleet's submarines, lies across the pier from

7–42. Three aircraft meet light American AA fire.

7–43. Lt. Comdr. Takeshige Egusa.

7–44. Lt. Howell M. Forgy, chaplain, *New Orleans*.

7–45. The Navy Yard at about 0915.

7–46. *Neosho* arrives from Ford Island.

7–47. A *kansen* from *Kaga* screams down over the Navy Yard and submarine base.

7–48. Damage to the pier alongside *Honolulu*. The entry hole in the dock wall is circled.

Narwahl. Neosho arrives from Ford Island fresh from her encounter with Chihaya's aircraft and is seeking the relative safety of the Navy Yard. At 0930 she hove to the wharf at Merry Point, just astern of *Castor*. Photo **7–47** shows a *kansen* from *Kaga* plunging down during an attack over the Navy Yard and submarine base.

By 0915, *Honolulu* stood ready to leave the Navy Yard. She could not complete preparations to sortie, for at 0920 a dive-bomber piloted by Sea1c. Motomu Kato from *Soryu* bore down on her from the southeast. Kato aimed his bomb well. The missile struck the pier alongside *Honolulu*, penetrated the dock wall, and exploded underneath the ship. The explosion buckled *Honolulu*'s hull and put her out of action until 12 January 1942. The bomb not only damaged *Honolulu* but also blew away the fenders (cushioning timbers) from the face of the dock (**7–48**).

Final Events and the End of the Raid

Arizona burns at the northern end of Battleship Row (**7–49**). The stern section, still buoyant and relatively intact, remained above the surface, and the machine guns in platform atop the mainmast stood ready to meet any new threat. *West Virginia* was sunk but upright, thanks to the counterflooding initiated early in the attack (**7–50**). Fires plagued her during the second wave and burned well into the evening. *Tennessee* appeared to be intact, although hit by two bombs. Burning oil drifting down from *Arizona* posed

7–49. *Arizona* afire.

7–50. *West Virginia* (outboard of *Tennessee*) lies sunk but upright. Note the overturned hull of *Oklahoma* at left.

a serious threat to other vessels. In **7–51**, a rescuer poised on a launch casts a lifeline to a swimmer beside the burning *West Virginia*, while personnel on the upper level of the superstructure near the battleship's foremast are trapped. *West Virginia*'s fire cast a pall of smoke over *Maryland*, inboard the stricken *Oklahoma* (**7–52**).

As oil fires crept closer to *California*, the Pacific Fleet had one of its few bright moments of the morning. At 0931, Capt. George A. Rood (**7–53**) got *St. Louis* under way from her berth in the repair basin. In **7–54**, she heads out to sea at about 0940, while off her starboard quarter, *Bagley* is likewise under way, still backing up the channel after leaving her berth in the Navy Yard. *St. Louis* narrowly missed becoming a casualty by evading a torpedo fired from one of the midget submarines lurking outside the harbor's entrance channel.

7–53. Capt. George A. Rood, circa 1940.

7–51. A rescuer throws a lifeline to a swimmer near *West Virginia*. Note the CXAM-1 "bedspring" radar antenna atop the foremast.

7–52. Smoke from *West Virginia* partially obscures *Maryland.* This photo illustrates the difficulties AA gun crews faced during the attack.

7–54. *St. Louis* makes the turn around the Navy Yard, headed out to sea.

As smoke overhung Battleship Row, *California* listed from two torpedo hits and also suffered from a bomb that set her on fire amidships (**7–55**). Shortly after 0930, burning oil threatened *California*'s stern (**7–56**). It seriously interfered with efforts to keep the battleship afloat, and indeed official sources cited the oil fires as the ultimate cause of the ship's damage. As the oil closes in, several men in mufti, probably officers returning from leave, can be seen disembarking from a launch in **7–57**.

7–55. From Ford Island's control tower east, smoke hides Battleship Row at left. At right, *California* lists from two torpedoes and one bomb.

7–56. Burning oil laps at *California*'s stern.

7–57. Interfering with efforts to keep *California* afloat, burning oil closes in on her stern.

Shortly before 1000, an inferno engulfed *California*; personnel in a launch off her port bow look on helplessly in **7–58**. At 1002, on the captain's order, the crew abandoned ship (**7–59**), but within minutes the order was rescinded, and the men began returning to try to keep her afloat. In photo **7–60**, the ship vanishes in smoke and flame as the yard tug *Nokomis* arrives on the scene to lend assistance.

7–58. Fire engulfs *California*.

7–59. *California*'s crew abandons ship.

7–60. *California* disappears behind a proscenium of smoke and flame.

7–61. *Oglala* falls toward TenTen Pier.

7–63. *Phoenix* on her way to join Task Force One.

Oglala commenced capsizing to port at about 0930, her hull ruptured by the pressure wave from *Helena*'s torpedo hit (**7–61**). Listing 45°, *Oglala* fell inward toward TenTen Pier. By 1000, she finally collapsed onto her port side and came to rest in the Pearl Harbor mud with a 90° list. Photo **7–62** was taken shortly thereafter, at about 1020, as *Jarvis* backed out of Berth No. 6 in the Navy Yard.

Assisted by harbor tug *VT–152*, *Phoenix* (CL–46) got under way at 1010 and attempted to sortie via the north channel; however, after receiving orders to remain inside the harbor, she returned to Berth C–6. Under way once again after 1100, she sortied via the south channel to join Task Force One outside the harbor. *Phoenix* passed the burning wreckage of Battleship Row at 1136 (**7–63**). Her track chart documents the confusion and complications the vessel encountered as she attempted to sortie (**7–64**). Even with yardcraft assistance, the cruiser's passage, to and fro, through Pearl Harbor's cramped moorings was a tedious, time-consuming ordeal.

7–62. By 1000, *Oglala* collapsed onto her port side. *Jarvis* is circled at left.

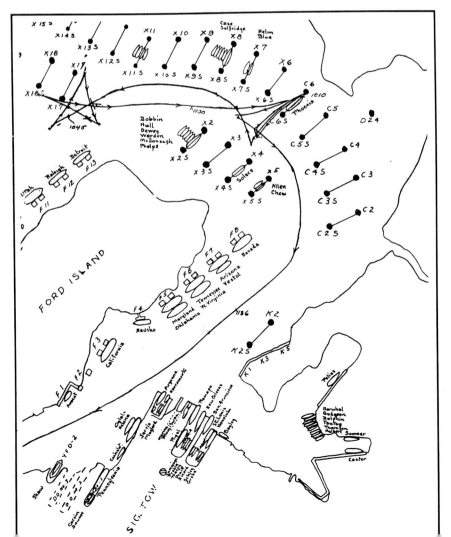

7–64. *Phoenix*'s track chart from 7 December.

Braving bombs and bullets, a host of small launches and boats labored throughout the attack and afterward to rescue swimmers from the water. In **7–65**, a launch pulls parallel to *Oklahoma* and *Maryland* after a run through the waters adjacent to Battleship Row. A large assortment of small craft scoured the area abreast *West Virginia* and plucked up sailors as they abandoned the big ship (**7–66**). In **7–67**, a launch travels northeast searching for swimmers from *Arizona* after the attack.

7–65. A rescue motor launch reaching *Oklahoma* and *Maryland.*

7–66. Small craft rescue sailors abandoning *West Virginia.*

7–67. A launch searches for swimmers off _Arizona's_ port bow. Note the light gray form of the retired cruiser _Baltimore_ (right).

A sorry spectacle indeed greeted any American looking at Battleship Row in the wake of the raid (**7–68**). The sight of the American battle line prostrate with its heart torn out had a devastating effect on the Pacific Fleet's morale. The panoramic view in **7–69** shows Pearl Harbor from the northeast just as the raid ended. Several details confirm the time of this photograph as roughly 1000 to 1030: Because no flak bursts soil the sky, the photograph was taken after the raid's conclusion. *Nevada* lies beached on Hospital Point, which times the picture no later than 1030. Left of *Nevada*, smoke mushrooms out of *Shaw* in the floating drydock, and dense smoke enshrouds much of Battleship Row. *California* lists to port, her foremast visible in the small bright patch at the center of the enormous pall hanging over the battleships. Oil fires, clearing away from *California*, burn just to the left of the ship. Much of the smoke in the photo rolls out of *Arizona* at the north end of Battleship Row. *Vestal* lies beached on Aiea Shoal.

7–68. Battleship Row some time after noon.

7–69. Pearl Harbor from the northeast, soon after the raid ended. Note *Nevada* beached at center.

The Airfields During the Second Wave

Pearl Harbor Naval Air Station

The confusion and destruction at Ford Island are evident in **7–70**, a vista from the island's water tower late in the second wave: Gutted and still in flames from the initial dive-bombing attack, Hangar 6 dominates the scene. Wreckage from several PBYs litters the pavement, and OS2U–3 floatplanes have been deposited by the battleships upon coming into port. Behind Hangar 6, Navy personnel have begun sweeping debris in **7–71**. On the southwest corner of Ford Island, smoke from Battleship Row rose behind the aircraft of Utility Squadron 2 (VJ–2), which included three Grumman J2F Duck amphibians and a PBY-1 (**7–72**).

7–70. NAS Pearl Harbor as seen from Ford Island's water tower.

7–71. Sailors start cleaning up.

7–72. Smoke from Battleship Row.

Hickam Field

Twenty-seven *kanko* under the command of Lt. Comdr. Shigekazu Shimazaki (**7–73**), leader of *Zuikaku*'s horizontal bombing unit and overall leader of the second-wave attack, completed the destruction at Hickam. *Akagi*'s second-wave fighters, under Lt. Saburo Shindo, continued the strafing attacks at Hickam.

Perhaps more than any other, photograph **7–74** shows Pearl Harbor as the Japanese remembered it. The photo looks northeast from a *kanko* of the second wave piloted by Shimazaki's wingman, WO Harunari Yaegashi. In it, aircraft E11–307 from *Zuikaku*—manned by Sea1c. Masato Hatanaka (pilot), P02c. Hideichi Kamino (observer), and Sea1c. Kingoro Oizumi (radioman)—heads south, ready to return to its carrier. Smoke hides much of Battleship Row. Some details are visible, however: the overturned hull of *Oklahoma*, the listing *California*, *Vestal* beached on Aeia

Shoal. *Neosho* has just arrived in the Navy Yard, and her screws churn up a telltale wake. Smoke mushrooms out of the drydock areas from destroyers *Cassin*, *Downes*, and *Shaw*. Beneath the Kate's cowling, a destroyer opposite Waipio Peninsula charges down the entrance channel. Smoke rises from various points along Hickam's hangar line, and oil trucks in a storage area behind the hangars are also in flames.

Amid the confusion, death, and destruction, the sight of the American flag still flying undoubtedly stirred many American hearts. The bullet-ridden Stars and Stripes at Hickam most effectively conveyed the words of Francis Scott Key: "Our flag was still there." The photographer of **7–75** was looking south from Hickam's parade ground toward the burning Hale Makai aircrew barracks. In **7–76**, a B–17D Flying Fortress of the Eleventh Bombardment Wing burns itself out on Hickam's apron. During the attack, Hickam's streets and avenues became a nightmarish, smoke-filled maze. Choking the horizon, thick smoke

7–74. Pearl Harbor as the Japanese remembered it.

7–73. Lt. Comdr. Shigekazu Shimazaki.

7–75. " . . . Our flag was still there. . . ."

7–76. A B-17D burns on Hickam Field's apron.

boiled up in the distance (7–77), not only from the hangar line but also from oil trucks burning beyond the barracks, which were themselves afire. In 7–78, the photographer was looking south from the parade ground at Hickam, possibly during the lull. Fires burned in the aircrew barracks following Japanese aircraft attacks, and American casualties were very heavy in that area, as the Japanese machine-gunned the barracks repeatedly. The building also received several direct bomb hits.

7–77. View looking southwest from the Hickam Parade Ground.

7–78. The aircrew barracks at Hickam.

Wheeler Field

According to Maj. Gen. Howard C. Davidson, commanding the Fourteenth Pursuit Wing, Wheeler "did not have very much of a second-wave attack." As far as the authors can determine, the dive-bombers that did hit Wheeler during the second wave were from *Kaga*. Among other actions, they tried to shoot up two P–40s that were loading ammunition, but the two pilots, Lt. Kenneth M. Taylor and Lt. George S. Welch, took off safely and continued their mission. (See "U.S. Army Fighter Activity.")

In photo **7–79**, ground personnel service one of Wheeler's P–36As in front of the hangar line. The aircraft's ammunition hatches stand open on the wings and engine cowling, and a tire is being changed. The authors have been unable to determine whether this photograph was taken during the raid or just after it.

7–79. Ground crews at Wheeler service a P–36A in front of Hangar 2.

Ewa MCAS

Although engine trouble prevented Lt. Michio Koba-yashi, leader, *Hiryu* dive-bombers (7–80), from accompanying his unit, his men acquitted themselves well, not only against ships in Pearl Harbor but also in executing a strafing attack on Ewa. By the time that Japanese fighters and dive-bombers broke off their strafing and departed from Ewa at the end of the second wave, no aircraft were available at that facility for immediate use. In 7–81, a Vindicator scout bomber lies burned and broken on Ewa's parking apron; in 7–82, an SBD Dauntless is likewise collapsed and burning on the apron. Comparatively few transport aircraft were available to the military on Oahu before the war. Photo 7–83 shows burning gasoline destroying one of them, a JO–2 at Ewa.

7–80. Lt. Michio Kobayashi.

7–82. An SBD burning on Ewa's apron.

7–81. An SB2U-3 demolished on Ewa's parking apron.

7–83. Burning gasoline consumes this Lockheed JO-2 transport (BuNo 1051) at Ewa.

The Marines at Ewa fought with any weapons at their disposal. Two of the men, Pvt. William G. Turner (7–84) and M. Sgt. Emil S. Peters (7–85), jumped into the rear cockpit of a spare SBD–2 (7–86) parked behind the VMSB–232 tents. They unshipped the rear gun and commenced shooting at the Japanese aircraft, with Peters firing the gun and Turner feeding the ammunition. Although both men were wounded, they managed to shoot down one of the attackers. Private Turner later died of his wounds. Both men received the Bronze Star for their bravery under fire.

During the attack on Ewa, an ambulance (7–87) provided cover for Navy Pharmacist's Mate Orin D. Smith. When the raid began, he was on duty at the base dispensary. Smith joined the driver, Pfc. James W. Mann, in the ambulance and headed straight for the burning aircraft. Strafing planes soon forced the two men to retreat under their vehicle, where Smith was wounded. The Japanese shot fifty-two holes through the ambulance.

7–84. Pvt. William G. Turner, USMC.

7–85. M. Sgt. Emil S. Peters, USMC.

7–86. A bullet-ridden SBD-2 (BuNo 2111) parked at Ewa.

7–87. Ewa's 1938 Ford ambulance.

NAS Kaneohe Bay

Eighteen horizontal bombers from *Shokaku* under Lt. Tatsuo Ichihara struck Kaneohe. After strafing Bellows Field, *Soryu*'s second-wave fighters, under Lt. Fusata Iida (7–88), along with nine fighters from *Hiryu* under Lt. Sumio Nono (7–89), descended upon Kaneohe. Iida died there, victim of an American sailor's Browning automatic rifle fire. Lt. (jg) Iyozo Fujita took over and led the *Soryu* fighters toward Wheeler but never reached there. His men became involved in dogfights, and he led the survivors directly back to their carrier.

Japanese bombers struck hard at Kaneohe during the second wave. While Iida's fighters strafed the base, two divisions of *kanko* from *Shokaku* pummeled Kaneohe from 6,500 feet. A crewman in one of the aircraft recorded the bombing run for posterity with a motion picture camera. In 7–90, motion picture frames form a panorama of the Japanese bombing run, including the framework of a new hangar under construction and a pattern of bomb blasts splotching its way down the asphalt parking apron. All of the bombs were misses, although several of the PBYs would catch fire later. Wreckage of several aircraft that were damaged or destroyed during previous attacks is also in evidence. In 7–91, *Shokaku*'s *kanko* EI–329 flies past Kaneohe with empty bomb crutches after completing its bomb run, while smoke climbs out to the north from the smoldering aircraft on Kaneohe's ramp. Farther out to the east, the whole of NAS Kaneohe Bay, including a new runway, was spread out before Japanese eyes (7–92).

7–88. Lt. Fusata Iida.   **7–89. Lt. Sumio Nono.**

7–90. Second-wave Japanese bombers attack Kaneohe.

7–91. *Shokaku's kanko* EI-329 at Kaneohe Bay.

7–92. Japanese view of NAS Kaneohe.

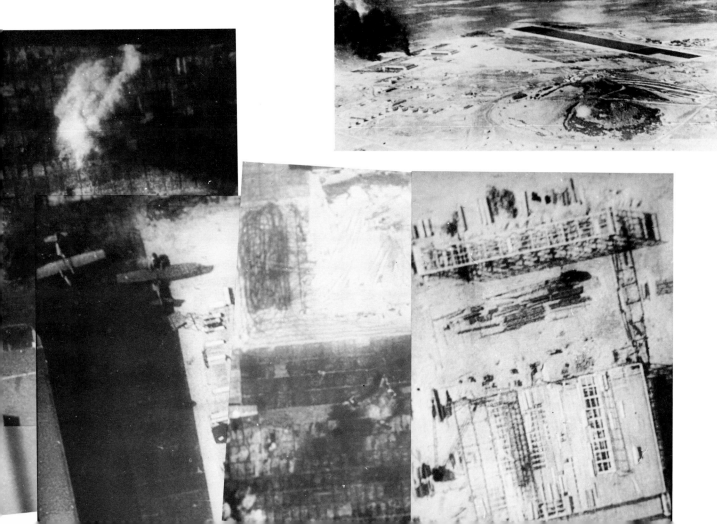

U.S. Army Fighter Activity

American aerial opposition to the Japanese was scant but spirited and determined. The handful of Hawaiian Air Force pilots who managed to get airborne accounted for about 50 percent of Japanese losses over Oahu.

Haleiwa Field

The Americans took off—or tried to take off—in three distinct groups. The most successful were five pilots from the Forty-Seventh Pursuit Squadron who survived a wild ride in two separate cars up from Wheeler Field, where they had spent the night, to Haleiwa Field, where their squadron was training. Just enough aircraft were available—five P–40s and a P–36A. These five fliers accounted for as many as seven aircraft. The most successful, 2d Lt. Kenneth M. Taylor (7–93, two victories) and 2d Lt. George S. Welch (7–94, four victories), took off first and engaged the enemy over Ewa and Wahialua. In 7–95, Taylor and Welch, both awarded the Distinguished Service Cross, pose for a photographer during the awards ceremony at Wheeler on 9 January 1942.

Three other individuals became airborne soon after: 2d Lt. Harry W. Brown (7–96, one victory), 1st Lt. Robert J. Rodgers (7–97), and 2d Lt. John L. Dains (7–98). Dains, who flew three sorties, perished in a crash at Schofield Barracks, tragically shot down by American AA fire. First Lt. John J. Webster (7–99) also took off from Haleiwa and later joined Rodgers and Brown in a wild melee off Kaena Point.

7–96. 1st Lt. Harry W. Brown.

7–97. 1st Lt. Robert J. Rodgers.

7–98. 2d Lt. John L. Dains.

7–99. 1st Lt. John J. Webster.

7–93. 2d Lt. Kenneth M. Taylor.

7–94. 2d Lt. George S. Welch.

7–95. 2d Lt. George Welch and 2d Lt. Kenneth ("Hominy") Taylor (nicknamed for his hometown in Oklahoma).

Bellows Field

In action on Oahu's eastern shore, Iida's *kansen* from *Soryu* bounced three Americans attempting to take off from Bellows Field between 0855 and 0900. The Japanese machine-gunned and killed 2d Lt. Hans C. Christiansen (7–100) as he climbed into his P–40. The other two pilots, 2d Lt. George A. Whiteman (7–101) and 2d Lt. Samuel W. Bishop (7–102), barely managed to leave the runway at Bellows before being shot down. Whiteman crashed into the beach at Bellows while Bishop, the only survivor of the trio, plunged into the ocean and swam back to the field. In photograph 7–103, Bishop poses in the cockpit of a P–40. The aircraft, assigned to the Nineteenth Pursuit Squadron at the time of the raid, lay in first-echelon maintenance at Wheeler Field.

7–100. 2d Lt. Hans C. Christiansen.

7–101. 2d Lt. George A. Whiteman.

7–103. Second Lieutenant Bishop, the sole survivor of the Bellows trio, poses in the cockpit of another survivor of the raid, P-40B, serial 41-13308.

Wheeler Field

At 0850, a group of pilots from the Forty-Sixth Squadron took off in their P–36As under the leadership of 1st Lt. Lewis M. Sanders (7–104) and battled Iida's fighters off Kaneohe. Among them were 2d Lt. Gordon H. Sterling (7–105) and 2d Lt. John Thacker (7–106). Later, 2d Lt. Malcolm A. Moore (7–107) took off, as did 2d Lt. Othneil ("Mike") Norris (7–108). Sanders and Sterling were both credited with kills, but Sterling's fighter plunged into Kaneohe Bay.

7–102. 2d Lt. Samuel W. Bishop.

7–105. 2d Lt. Gordon H. Sterling.

7–107. 2d Lt. Malcolm A. Moore.

7–108. 2d Lt. Othneil Norris.

7–106. 2d Lt. John M. Thacker.

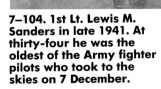

7–104. 1st Lt. Lewis M. Sanders in late 1941. At thirty-four he was the oldest of the Army fighter pilots who took to the skies on 7 December.

Fingers crossed, 2d Lt. Philip M. Rasmussen (**7–109**) stands beside the P–36A in which he engaged Japanese fighters over Kaneohe (**7–110**). Twenty-millimeter cannon fire heavily damaged his aircraft in the fuselage and wings (**7–111**). Gunfire likewise severed his rudder cable (**7–112**). In **7–113** are five of the day's heroes, wearing their decorations: Harry W. Brown (Silver Star), Philip M. Rasmussen (Silver Star), Lewis M. Sanders (Silver Star), Kenneth M. Taylor (Purple Heart), and John J. Webster (Silver Star, Purple Heart).

7–109. 2d Lt. Philip M. Rasmussen as an air cadet, circa 1940.

7–110. 2d Lt. Philip M. Rasmussen stands beside his P-36A, serial 38-86. Note the holes in the fuselage.

7–111. The ground crews at Wheeler counted 544 bullet and shell holes in Rasmussen's P-36A.

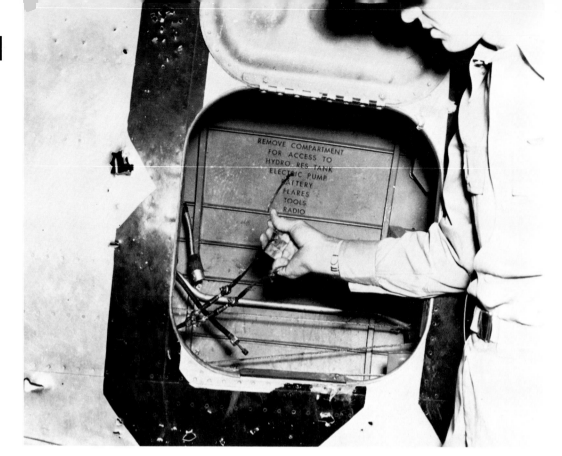

7–112. Rasmussen holds up his plane's severed rudder cables.

7–113. Five Army fighter pilots stand at Wheeler Field on 1 July 1942 after being decorated for their actions against the Japanese.

7–114. *Shokaku's* **kanko begin the long journey back to the ship after bombing NAS Kaneohe Bay.**

7–115. **A kanko prepares to land on *Akagi*. Note the destroyer on plane guard duty astern the carrier.**

Japanese Return to the Carriers

Eventually, their mission fulfilled, the Japanese headed back to their mother carriers. They used the area off Kaena Point, west of Oahu, as a rendezvous point before starting the long flight north. In photograph 7–114, *kanko* of the second-wave attack wend their way back to *Shokaku*; in 7–115, a *kanko* from the first wave prepares to touch down on *Akagi*. Battle-damaged aircraft, the long return flight, fatigue, and frayed nerves took a toll, with a number of bad landings. Occasionally, deck crews pushed overboard air-

7–116. A *kansen* touches down onto *Akagi*'s flight deck and heads for the barriers forward after missing the arrestor wires aft. Note fire-fighting equipment in front of the islands.

7–117. Incoming bombers continue to return to *Akagi*.

7–118. An exhausted airman on *Akagi*.

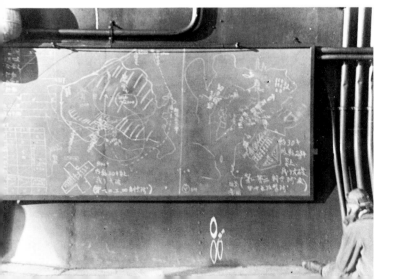

craft with extensive damage. In **7–116,** a *kansen* floats down onto *Akagi*'s flight deck, as observers crowd the carrier's island to watch the landings. Photo **7–117** shows Japanese bombers continuing to return to *Akagi*. The heavy cables are used to snare the arrester hooks mounted on the underside of each aircraft. In **7–118,** an exhausted airman aboard *Akagi* collapses in front of the carrier's island; the blackboard displays a rough map of the area around Pearl Harbor, including the airfields at Hickam and Ewa.

F4F Flight from Enterprise

Sunset did not end the commotion in the skies over Oahu. At 2110, six F4F Wildcats from *Enterprise* droned over the harbor. They were all low on fuel because of an unintended detour toward Molokai. Just as the six pilots lowered their gear and entered a landing pattern for Ford Island, the entire harbor opened fire. Miraculously, two of the pilots were able to land safely on Ford Island, and a third made Barbers Point before bailing out. However, three of the little band from *Enterprise* perished under the fire of their own fleet. Among them was the flight leader, Lt. (jg) Fritz Hebel (7–119), who made a forced landing near Wheeler but died of a fractured skull.

The aircraft piloted by Ens. Herbert H. Menges (7–120) caught fire and crashed onto Pearl City's Palm Lodge, northeast of the harbor. In the confusion following the raid, Menges's shattered body was not recovered until 11 December. Although Lt. (jg) Eric Allen, Jr. (7–121), hit the silk over the harbor, he died of internal injuries suffered as a result of his low-altitude bailout.

7–119. Lt. (jg) Fritz Hebel.

7–120. Ens. Herbert H. Menges.

7–121. Lt. (jg) Eric Allen, Jr.

CHAPTER 8

Panorama of Destruction

In the immediate aftermath of the attack, it would have been difficult, if not impossible, to find anyone on Oahu who could have given a factual account of what happened, let alone a reasonable assessment of the results from the American standpoint. Rumors proliferated and were widely believed, for example: (1)A third wave had attacked. This nonexistent event showed up in ships' logs, sworn testimony, and eyewitness accounts. (2) The local Japanese had committed widespread sabotage. This possibility had been a long-standing obsession with many of Oahu's top defenders. No such sabotage occurred, but belief that it had happened rose as far up the ladder as Secretary of the Navy Frank Knox. (3) Japanese troop transports were off Barbers Point, and (4) Japanese paratroops were landing. These and similar wild tales kept the military and civilians alike confused and on edge.

Anyone surveying the scene the Japanese had left behind might well have assumed that the U.S. Pacific Fleet and the Hawaiian Air Force had sustained a mortal blow. *Nevada*, having moved to Buoy No. 19, had her stern jammed into the mud on Waipo Peninsula. She was down by her bow, still burning. The yard tug *Hoga*, having pushed *Nevada* across the channel, played water on her fires (**8–1**).

8–1. *Nevada* at Pearl Harbor Channel Buoy 19.

California gradually settled for several days. In **8–2**, the submarine rescue vessel *Widgeon* and seaplane tender *Swan* stand by her. Eventually she hit bottom and was officially considered sunk. *Maryland* had suffered relatively light damage, but her berthmate, *Oklahoma*, had capsized to within 20° or 30° of being upside down (**8–3**). *West Virginia* had also come to rest on the bottom and was considered sunk. In **8–4** the garbage lighter *YG–17* plays water on the battleship's fires, while small craft search for survivors. Next to *West Virginia*, *Tennessee* had taken two bomb hits. The

8–2. *California,* tended by *Widgeon* and *Swan,* is very low in the water but not yet on the harbor bottom.

8–3. A rescue party stands on the forward portion of *Oklahoma*'s upturned hull on 8 December.

8—4. Garbage lighter *YG-17* sprays *West Virginia* amidships.

8–5. At left, the minesweeper *Tern* (in front) and *Hoga* (behind) lie off *Arizona*'s port bow during 9 December. *Solace* is in the center of the background.

8–6. Drydock No. 1 after the attack. *Pennsylvania* lies behind *Cassin* (right) and *Downes* (left).

8–7. Fleet tug *Sunnadin* (AT-48) tends the cruiser *Raleigh.*

8–8. Lt. Comdr. Raymond C. Tellin, circa 1950.

nearby *Arizona* continued to burn until 9 December (**8–5**). Damaged by a single bomb, *Pennsylvania* lay in Drydock No. 1, where ahead of her, *Cassin* had fallen against *Downes* (**8–6**).

In the midafternoon of 7 December, the fleet tug *Sunnadin* secured a pontoon stowage barge to *Raleigh* as an emergency flotation device (**8–7**). *Raleigh* provided volunteers to join *Utah* survivors in forming a rescue party, led by Carpenter R. C. Tellin (**8–8**). They succeeded in rescuing several men from the capsized *Utah* (**8–9**).

8–9. A rescue party, led by Carpenter R. C. Tellin, stands on *Utah*'s hull.

In addition, the attack had left other victims: *Shaw* continued to burn furiously after her spectacular explosion (8–10). *Helena* had sustained heavy damage, and *Oglala* lay on her side, nearly touching TenTen Pier. *Honolulu* had been damaged. *Curtiss* had been set on fire when the Japanese aircraft crashed her, and a bomb had also caused considerable wreckage. Two bombs had damaged *Vestal*, which beached at Aiea. Dense smoke hung over the entire scene, while small boats plying the oily waters attempted to rescue the living and recover the dead.

A tour of the airfields would have revealed no cause for optimism. Hickam had taken a particularly heavy beating. Not everyone there was as fortunate as S. Sgt. Dean Morris, safely reunited with his wife (8–11). Of fifty-six bombers on hand, thirty-eight remained, of which nineteen were out of commission. In **8–12** is the crumpled wreckage of a B–18 outside Hangar 15, which sustained major damage. A

8–11. S. Sgt. Dean Morris reunited with his wife at Hickam Field after the attack.

8–10. The destroyer *Shaw* burns out of control in *YFD-2*. Note that the drydock is only partially sunk, listing at about 25°.

8–12. A burned B-18 lies just outside Hangar 15.

direct hit wrecked Hangar 11, shown in **8–13** with a smashed B–18. The interior of Hangar 7 was a shambles. Technical facilities also suffered, which hampered salvage efforts. Broken water mains seriously interfered with fire fighting (**8–14**), as did Japanese destruction of the fire-house and engines. A Kate from *Zuikaku* scored a direct hit, smashing windows and venetian blinds, on the third floor of the Hale Makai Aircrew Barracks. Nearly every wall of the barracks bore the marks of shrapnel and machine-gun fire (**8–15**). The crowded mess hall took a bomb hit early

8–13. A direct hit gutted Hangar 11. The tail of Brig. Gen. Jacob Rudolph's battered personal B-18 protrudes into the photo at right.

8–15. A wide-angle view of the Hale Makai Aircrew Barracks.

8–14. On Hangar Avenue, past Hangar 11 at left, water stands in the street and surrounding area from a ruptured water main.

in the raid that produced many casualties; the presence of the survivors is not evident in photograph **8–16**.

Wheeler experienced comparable damage. Forty of its 140 fighters had been destroyed, and fifty-three put out of commission. In **8–17** four P–40s lie heaped on the east end of the parking apron. Other aircraft wreckage is piled at Hangar 3 in **8–18**. The expression on Capt. George S. Boyer's face was typical of American reaction to this destruction (**8–19**). Tons of rubble marked the spot where a

8–16. Many of the barracks' casualties occurred in the crowded mess hall.

8–17. The remains of four Seventy-Third Pursuit Squadron P-40s.

8–19. Capt. George S. Boyer, U.S. Army Medical Corps. Anger and determination on his features.

8–18. Bulldozed wreckage on the apron near Hangar 3.

first-wave *kanbaku* scored a direct hit on the Seventy-Fifth Service Squadron barracks (8–20). The Japanese even shot up General Davidson's 1941 Ford (8–21).

Bellows escaped relatively lightly. Only two of its aircraft were destroyed, and four were put out of commission. One of Bellow's casualties, a gasoline truck, was hit when Nono's fighters strafed it (8–22). A disabled fighter is pictured in 8–23, and another suffered a missing propeller and a collapsed undercarriage (8–24).

8–21. Machine-gun fire riddled Brig. Gen. Howard C. Davidson's 1941 Ford "Fordor" sedan.

8–20. Just to the rear of the hangar line, rubble marks the site of a direct hit.

8–23. A forlorn P-40C, victim of Japanese cannon fire, rests on Bellows's sandy ground.

8–22. The burned-out hulk of a strafed gasoline truck on the southern side of Bellows's runway.

8–24. Another hapless P-40 at Bellows.

At Ewa, aircraft losses were heavy—thirty-three planes of fifty-one. One of them was the gutted Vindicator in 8–25, set on fire by strafers. For some reason, strafers at Ewa concentrated on private cars like the battle-scarred 1937 LaSalle in 8–26. Among the wounded personnel was T. Sgt. Henry H. Anglin, in 8–27 shown holding a Japanese bullet.

Nowhere was aircraft destruction as proportionately appalling as at Kaneohe. Of thirty-seven planes, twenty-eight were lost. Hangar 1, with the planes therein, was completely destroyed. Fire fighting was extremely difficult, as strafers put Kaneohe's only fire truck out of action early in the attack (8–28). Pathetic evidence of Kaneohe's hopes

8–25. A burned-out SB2U-3 from VMSB-231 on the asphalt at Ewa.

8–27. Standing in front of Ewa's dispensary, base photographer T. Sgt. Henry H. Anglin holds up a Japanese 7.7-millimeter bullet.

DISPENSARY
SICK CALL HOURS
0800 1800 DAILY

8–28. Strafing Japanese fighters disabled Kaneohe Bay's only fire truck, a 1939 Seagrave pumper. The fire station is visible in the background at far left.

8–26. This 1937 LaSalle two-door touring sedan, charred and blistered, lies near Ewa's parking lot.

of fighting back is the glimpse in **8–29** of five sailors manning two machine guns in a bomb crater. Attempts to salvage a PBY are also under way (**8–30**).

Ford Island lost twenty-six of sixty-five aircraft, mostly PBYs. Photo **8–31** shows the hapless condition of some of these planes. Hangar 6 was set on fire; its office area and

8–29. Five sailors man two Browning machine guns (a .30 caliber and a .50 caliber) in a bomb crater at Kaneohe.

8–31. Wreckage of several PBYs on the seaplane ramp in front of Hangar 6.

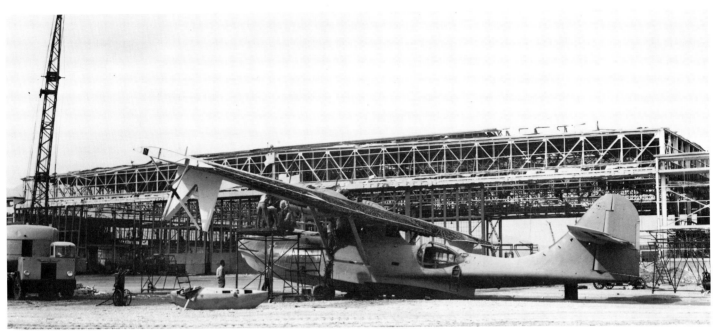

8–30. Salvagers erect scaffolding under the wing of a PBY-5.

east wing lost most of their windows. A collapsed OS2U–3 rested in front of the office (8–32). Of course, much unsightly and dangerous debris washed ashore on Ford Island (8–33).

Even the city of Honolulu suffered considerable damage and some casualties. The citizens did not know that their troubles came, not from the Japanese, but from so-called friendly fire caused by defective ammunition and inexperienced gun crews. Bystanders joined Honolulu's firemen to control the blaze at Lunalilo School (8–34). In some cases

8–32. The office area at Hangar 6.

8–33. Flotsam, fuel oil, and refuse collect on the shore of Ford Island.

8–34. Honolulu's fire fighters and bystanders attempt to contain the blaze at Lunalilo School on Pumehaua Street.

8–35. Antiaircraft shells sometimes leveled entire structures, as shown here.

8–37. The "third extra" of the Honolulu *Star-Bulletin* on a civil defense worker's desk.

8–36. Paul Goo's demolished living room in his otherwise intact house.

entire buildings were demolished (8–35). As in any disaster, there were freak happenings. A Navy shell wrecked Paul Goo's living room but spared the rest of the dwelling (8–36). The newspapers kept the public abreast as best they could. In 8–37, a civil defense worker sits beside a copy of the Honolulu *Star-Bulletin* headlined "Martial Law Declared: Deaths Are Mounting."

Shortly after noon on Monday, 8 December 1941, the Congress of the United States met in joint session at the request of President Franklin Delano Roosevelt. He abandoned his wheelchair, stood at the podium to a storm of applause, and in a brief, stirring address asked "that the Congress declare that since the unprovoked and dastardly attack by Japan on Sunday, December 7, 1941, a state of war has existed between the United States and the Empire of Japan" (8–38). From that moment there would be no more hesitation, no more questioning, no faltering of the national will until the Pacific war ended in victory for the United States and its allies.

8–38. Attention is riveted to the rostrum as President Franklin D. Roosevelt denounces the infamy of the Japanese Empire and asks a joint session of Congress to declare a state of war.

Epilogue

Gradually the fact that matters could have been much worse on Oahu became evident. Foolishly, from their standpoint, the Japanese had left Pearl Harbor's tank farms and machine shops intact. Repair work could begin immediately, and the seaworthy ships would not be hobbled for lack of fuel. Almost miraculously, no ship had been sunk in the channel, so the Navy could continue to use Pearl Harbor. The waters of Pearl Harbor were so shallow that ships could be refloated that would have been a dead loss if the Japanese had caught them in the open sea or even in Lahaina Anchorage.

Then, too, the aircraft carriers had escaped the raid, and most of the cruisers, destroyers, and support ships and all the submarines were untouched. As the war progressed, the Japanese appeared to have kicked the U.S. Pacific Fleet upstairs—into a swift, mobile force.

However, such assessments took time. Meanwhile, the military establishment on Oahu buckled down to an awesome task of salvage. The Army had the easier portion, for reconstruction of buildings did not present as many problems as renovating the ships. The aircraft were another matter, and for a while all the damaged planes seemed to be beyond repair. The mechanics of the Hawaiian Air Force rose to the challenge, however, and in time 80 percent were salvaged.

The story of how sunken or damaged ships were brought back to life is a saga of skill, courage, and determination. The job took several years, but in the end the U.S. Navy had lost only three vessels—*Arizona*, *Oklahoma*, and *Utah*. Except for the fifty-eight valiant lives lost aboard her, *Utah* could be written off with few qualms. The old battleship had long outlived her usefulness for combat, and after due consideration her salvage was determined to be too costly in terms of time, labor, and funds. Some of her ordnance was removed, but she remains where she sank, a fitting tomb for her dead.

Oklahoma had to be righted and moved to clear her berth, although little hope was entertained of actually restoring the ship. Salvage was attempted but proved fruitless. She was decommissioned on 1 September 1944 and in December 1946 was sold for scrap. On 17 May 1947, en route under tow to the mainland, she encountered a storm and sank, to the great relief of the men who had served aboard her and loved her.

Arizona was obviously a hopeless case; however, much effort was expended in investigating her hull and in salvaging whatever could be put to use. The decision was made to remove those portions of the battleship that remained above water and to leave the rest of her in position, to become, like *Utah*, a tomb for her dead. A memorial structure was erected over her hull and dedicated on Memorial Day 1962.

Despite its serene loveliness, the *Arizona* Memorial is a disquieting reminder of the price a nation may be called upon to pay for smugness and unpreparedness.

APPENDIX A

Chronology of Events Prior to the Attack

1940

10 April—Fleet to Hawaii
June—Fall of France
Summer—Herron alert against "trans-Pacific raid"
August—U.S. breaks Purple code
September—Tripartite Pact
12 November—Taranto
November—Plan DOG (Europe first)

1941

7 January—Yamamoto writes Oikawa
23 January—Nomura sails for U.S.
26 or 27 January—Yamamoto meets with Onishi
27 January—Grew message about rumor
1 February—Kimmel becomes CinC US
1 February—ONI places "no credence in Grew message"
7 February—Short becomes CG, Hawaiian Dept.
Early February—Genda becomes tactical planner of Pearl Harbor (PH) attack
27 March—ABC-1 agreement (strategy *if* U.S. enters war)
31 March—Martin-Bellinger Report sent to D.C.
10 April—FDR draws patrol line in Atlantic
            —First Air Fleet formed
19–22 May—About a quarter of Pacific Fleet transferred to Atlantic
22 June—Germany invades Russia
2 July—Imperial Conference
16 July—Konoye resigns, forms new cabinet
26 July—U.S. freezes Japanese assets
1 August—U.S. embargoes high-octane gas
7 August—FDR and party to Argentia
20 August—Farthing report to D.C.
11–16 September—War games for PH
24 September—Bomb plot message
9–13 October—Table maneuvers for PH
16 October—Konoye cabinet falls
18 October—Tojo becomes premier
18 October—Yamamoto threatens to resign, NGS submits

5 November—Togo gives Nomura deadline of 25 November
15 November—Kurusu arrives in U.S.
19 November—Winds message (East Wind Rain)
20 November—Japan presents Proposal B
21–25 November—Hull working on modus vivendi
21–26 November—Rendezvous at Hitokappu Bay
22 November—Togo extends deadline to 29th
26 November—Japanese fleet sighted headed for Indochina
            —Hull note
27 November—Kimmel and Short arrange to send fighter planes to Wake and Midway; *Enterprise* leaves
            —"War warning" messages to Kimmel and Short
            —Short initiates antisabotage alert
1 December—FDR tells Halifax GB can count on U.S. support
            —Imperial Conference officially decides on war
            —IJN changes call signals for second time in one month
2 December—CNO orders "three little ships" reconnaissance
            —Tokyo advises certain embassies and consulates to burn secret documents and destroy most codes
            —Climb Mt. Niitaka
3 December—CNO informs CinC PAC of code orders
            —"Kita message" (Kuehn's proposed code)
            —FDR tells Halifax GB can count on "armed support"
4 December—Nagumo orders sinking of enemy or neutral ships if necessary
5 December—*Lexington* leaves PH
6 December—First 13 parts of 14-part message
            —FDR writes Emperor
7 December—*Enterprise* due in PH
            —Budapest-Tokyo message
            —Brooke-Popham message
            —Part 14 received
            —"One o'clock" message
            —Marshall advises Short of one o'clock message

APPENDIX B

Japanese Air Unit Leaders

First Attack Wave

SHIP	Chutai (Div.)	Unit Commander	Aircraft	Targets Attacked

Horizontal Bombing Unit—Comdr. Mitsuo Fuchida— 49 B5N2—1 800-kg Armor-Piercing Bomb

SHIP	Chutai (Div.)	Unit Commander	Aircraft	Targets Attacked
AKAGI	1st	Comdr. Mitsuo Fuchida	5	Maryland
	2d	Lt. Goro Iwasaki	5	Tennessee/West Virginia
	3d	Lt. Izumi Furukawa	5	Tennessee/West Virginia
KAGA	1st	Lt. Comdr. Takashi Hashiguchi	5	Tennessee/West Virginia
	2d	Lt. Hideo Maki	5	Arizona/Vestal
	3d	Lt. Yoshitaka Mikami	4	Tennessee/West Virginia
SORYU	1st	Lt. Heijiro Abe	5	Tennessee/West Virginia
	2d	Lt. (jg) Sadao Yamamoto	5	Nevada
HIRYU	1st	Lt. Comdr. Tadashi Kusumi	5	Arizona
	2d	Lt. (jg) Toshio Hashimoto	5	California

Torpedo Bombing Unit—Lt. Comdr. Shigeharu Murata—40 B5N2—800-kg Torpedo

SHIP	Chutai (Div.)	Unit Commander	Aircraft	Targets Attacked
AKAGI	4th	Lt. Comdr. Shigeharu Murata	6	West Virginia/Oklahoma
	5th	Lt. Asao Negishi	6	California/West Virginia/Oklahoma
KAGA	1st	Lt. Kazuyoshi Kitajima	6	West Virginia/Oklahoma
	2d	Lt. Mimori Suzuki	6	West Virginia/Oklahoma/Nevada
SORYU	1st	Lt. Tsuyoshi Nagai	4	Helena/California/Utah
	2d	Lt. Tatsumi Nakajima	4	Utah/Raleigh
HIRYU	1st	Lt. Heita Matsumura	4	West Virginia/Oklahoma
	2d	Lt. Hiroharu Sumino	4	Helena

Dive-Bombing Unit—Lt. Comdr. Kakuichi Takahashi—51 D3A1—1 250-kg Land Bomb

SHIP	Chutai (Div.)	Unit Commander	Aircraft	Targets Attacked
SHOKAKU	3d	Lt. Comdr. Kakuichi Takahashi	9	NAS Pearl Harbor
	1st	Lt. Masao Yamaguchi	8	Hickam Field
	2d	Lt. Hisayoshi Fujita	9	Hickam Field
ZUIKAKU	1st	Lt. Akira Sakamoto	9	Wheeler Field
	2d	Lt. Tomatsu Ema	6 ?	Wheeler Field
	3d	Lt. C. Hayashi	10 ?	Wheeler Field

Fighter Unit—Comdr. Shigeru Itaya—43 A6M2—20-mm Cannon and 7.7-mm MG

SHIP	Chutai (Div.)	Unit Commander	Aircraft	Targets Attacked
AKAGI	2d	Lt. Comdr. Shigeru Itaya	9	Hickam Field/Ewa MACS
KAGA	1st	Lt. Yoshio Shiga	9	Hickam Field/Ewa MACS
SORYU	2d	Lt. Masaji Suganami	8	Wheeler Field/Ewa MACS
HIRYU	4th	Lt. Kiyokima Okajima	6	Wheeler Field/Ewa MACS
SHOKAKU	5th	Lt. Tadashi Kaneko	6	NAS Kaneohe Bay/Bellows Field
ZUIKAKU	6th	Lt. Masao Sato	5	NAS Kaneohe Bay

Second Attack Wave

SHIP	Chutai (Div.)	Unit Commander	Aircraft	Targets Attacked

Horizontal Bombing Unit—Lt. Comdr. Shigekazu Shimazaki—54 B5N2—2 250-kg Land Bombs* *or* **1 250-kg Land Bomb and 6 60-kg Ordinary Bombs****

SHIP	Chutai (Div.)	Unit Commander	Aircraft	Targets Attacked
SHOKAKU	1st	Lt. Tatsuo Ichihara	9	* NAS Kaneohe Bay
	2d	Lt. Tsutomu Hagiwara	9	* NAS Kaneohe Bay
	3d	Lt. Yoshiaki Ikuin	9	** NAS Pearl Harbor
ZUIKAKU	1st	Lt. Comdr. Shigekazu Shimazaki	9	* Hickam Field
	2d	Lt. Takemi Iwami	9	** Hickam Field
	3d	Lt. Yoshiaki Tsubota	9	** Hickam Field

Dive-Bombing Unit—Lt. Comdr. Takashige Egusa—78 D3A1— 1 250-kg Ordinary Bomb

SHIP	Chutai (Div.)	Unit Commander	Aircraft	Targets Attacked
AKAGI	1st	Lt. Takehiko Chihaya	9	NW Ford I, *Neosho, Shaw*
	2d	Lt. Zenji Abe	9	NW Ford I, *Maryland*
KAGA	1st	Lt. Saburo Makino	8	*Nevada*
	2d	Lt. Shoichi Ogawa	9	*West Virginia, Nevada, Maryland*
	3d	Lt. Shoichi Ibuki	9	*Nevada*
SORYU	1st	Lt. Comdr. Takashige Egusa	9	Navy Yard, *California, Dobbin*
	2d	Lt. Masatake Ikeda	8	Navy Yard, *California, Raleigh*
HIRYU	1st	Lt. Michio Kobayashi***	8	Navy Yard, *Helm, Maryland*
	2d	Lt. Shun Nakagawa	9	Navy Yard, *California, Maryland, West Virginia*

Fighter Unit—Lt. Saburo Shindo—35 A6M2—20-mm Cannon and 7.7-mm MG

SHIP	Chutai (Div.)	Unit Commander	Aircraft	Targets Attacked
AKAGI	1st	Lt. Saburo Shindo	9	Hickam Field
KAGA	2d	Lt. Yasushi Nikaido	9	Pearl Harbor
SORYU	3d	Lt. Fusata Iida	9	NAS Kaneohe Bay
HIRYU	4th	Lt. Sumio Nono	8	NAS Kaneohe Bay, Bellows Field

*** Totals exclude Lt. Kobayashi. Engine trouble prevented him from making the trip to Oahu.

Credits

Japanese Defense Agency, War History Section
(Boeicho Kenshujo Sensh Shitsu)
1–9, 2–7, 2–10, 6–106

Masataka Chihaya Collection
4–15, 4–23, 6–49

William M. Cleveland Collection
3–17, 6–52, 7–76 through 7–78, 8–12, 8–16

Robert J. Cressman Collection
5–22, 6–3, 6–75, 6–78, 6–79, 6–82, 6–84, 6–85,
6–89, 6–91, 7–119 through 7–121, 8–8

Egusa Family
7–43

Koku Fan Magazine
4–11, 5–1, 7–74

Claude A. Larkin Collection, Marine Historical
Center
3–24, 6–95, 7–81 through 7–83, 7–86, 7–87, 8–
25, 8–26

Walter Lord Collection
6–17

Mainichi Press Service
4–14, 5–27, 5–28, 6–107, 6–109, 6–110

Al Makiel Collection
2–34, 4–8, 4–9, 4–19, 5–4, 6–14, 6–60, 6–115,
7–92, 7–95, 7–115 through 7–118

Maru Magazine
2–1, 2–2, 2–6, 2–12, 2–13, 4–2 through 4–6, 4–
10, 4–13, 4–20, 4–21, 4–24, 5–3

National Archives
1–18, 2–14, 2–15, 2–19, 2–20, 2–22, 2–24 through
2–29, 2–31 through 2–33, 2–39 through 2–43, 2–
45 through 2–50, 3–1 through 3–7, 3–9, 3–11,
3–15, 3–18, 3–21, 3–23, 3–25 through 3–28, 4–
12, 4–17, 4–18, 5–5 through 5–12, 5–14, 5–23,
5–31, 5–33, 6–1, 6–5, 6–6, 6–12, 6–16, 6–20, 6–
21, 6–26 through 6–28, 6–32 through 6–34, 6–36,
6–42 through 6–44, 6–48, 6–54 through 6–57, 6–
62 through 6–74, 6–76, 6–81, 6–87, 6–88, 6–92
through 6–94, 6–96, 6–97, 6–99 through 6–102,
6–105, 6–108, 6–111 through 6–114, 7–3 through
7–6, 7–9 through 7–19, 7–21 through 7–23, 7–27
through 7–29, 7–31 through 7–42, 7–44 through

7–47, 7–49 through 7–52, 7–54 through 7–63, 7–
65 through 7–72, 7–90, 7–91, 7–93, 7–94, 7–96
through 7–102, 7–106 through 7–108, 8–1 through
8–5, 8–7, 8–9 through 8–11, 8–13 through 8–15,
8–17 through 8–24, 8–27 through 8–38

National Air & Space Museum
1–19 through 1–21, 2–35 through 2–38, 3–10, 3–
12 through 3–14, 3–16, 6–58, 6–59, 7–75, 7–103

Naval Historical Center
1–1, 1–8, 1–12 through 1–17, 2–4, 2–8, 2–11, 2–
21, 2–23, 2–30, 2–44, 2–51, 3–8, 3–20, 3–22, 5–
13, 5–15, 5–17 through 5–20, 5–24 through 5–26,
5–30, 6–2, 6–13, 6–30, 6–31, 6–35, 6–41, 6–47,
6–50, 6–51, 6–53, 6–90, 6–98, 6–104, 7–1, 7–2,
7–30, 7–48, 7–53, 7–80, 7–84, 7–85, 8–6

T. Nozawa Collection
2–16, 4–7, 4–16, 5–2, 7–114

Pearl Harbor Attack Hearings
4–1, 5–29, 5–32

Gordon W. Prange Collection
1–2 through 1–7, 1–10, 1–11, 2–9, 2–17, 4–25,
5–16, 6–4, 6–7 through 6–11, 6–15, 6–18, 6–19,
6–22 through 6–25, 6–37 through 6–40, 6–61, 6–
77, 7–7, 7–20, 7–73, 7–88, 7–89

Philip M. Rasmussen Collection
7–79, 7–109 through 7–112

Lewis M. Sanders Collection
7–104, 7–113

Sekai-No-Kansen Magazine
2–3, 2–5

Robert F. Sumrall Collection
5–21

Tomura Collection
4–22

United States Army Air Force
7–105

United States Navy
2–18, 6–29, 6–103, 7–8, 7–64

J. Michael Wenger Collection
6–45, 6–46, 6–80, 6–83, 6–86, 7–24 through 7–26

About the Authors

Donald M. Goldstein, Ph.D., Lieutenant Colonel, USAF (ret.), is associate professor of Public and International Affairs at the University of Pittsburgh. He lives with his family in Pittsburgh, Pennsylvania.

Katherine V. Dillon is a Chief Warrent Officer, USAF (ret.), and lives in Arlington, Virginia.

J. Michael Wenger, M.A., Duke University, is a freelance historian and lives with his family in Raleigh, North Carolina.